WATER, FIRE, WIND

The
Elements
of
Following
Christ

Bo
Cassell

Barefoot Ministries®
Kansas City, Missouri

Copyright 2007
by Bo Cassell and Barefoot Ministries®

ISBN 978-0-8341-5017-1

Printed in the United States of America

Editor: Rick Edwards
Assistant Editors: Stephanie McNelly and Stephanie Harris

Cover Design: Doug Bennett
Interior Design: Sharon R. Page

Library of Congress Cataloging-in-Publication Data

Cassell, Bo.
  Water, fire, wind : the elements of following Christ / by Bo Cassell.
    p. cm.
  ISBN 978-0-8341-5017-1
 1. Christian teenagers—Religious life. 2. Grace (Theology) 3. Holiness. 4. Spiritual formation. I. Title.

  BV4531.3.C38 2007
  248.8'3—dc22

2007017664

10 9 8 7 6 5 4 3 2 1

In memory of my grandfather, Basil Thomas Rogers,
whose character is written on the pages of my soul.

The author would like to acknowledge Dave Curtiss and Brian Hull—
whose vision of these elements and key questions provided the
starting point and direction of this book.

CONTENTS

Chapter One

THE WAY IS LOST

I don't want to be a "Christian" anymore.

Don't get me wrong. I believe in Jesus Christ. I love him with everything that is within me. I echo the beliefs of those who have gone before me . . .

I believe in God, the Father Almighty,
Maker of heaven and earth,
And in Jesus Christ, his only son, our Lord,
Who was conceived by the Holy Spirit,
Born of the Virgin Mary,
Suffered under Pontius Pilate,
Was crucified, dead, and buried.
He descended to the dead;
On the third day he rose again from the dead.
He ascended into heaven,
And sits at the right hand of God the Father Almighty.
From there he will come to judge the living and the dead.

I believe in the Holy Spirit,
The Holy Christian Church,
The communion of saints,
The forgiveness of sins,
The resurrection of the body,
And the life everlasting.
Amen![1]

But there's the problem. It is the power of that simple statement of belief that has me troubled. This creed represents a faith that is no longer captured by the word "Christian." So maybe this is a better way to say it:

I can't abide by the term "Christian" anymore.

I guess we could say that the term has lost its meaning, but that would be missing the point. The problem is not that the word has lost its meaning; the problem is that is has taken on a new meaning. The word has been hijacked. It no longer means what it is supposed to mean, and I can't live with that anymore. I don't identify with what "Christian" has come to mean. In fact, the idea of calling myself a Christian is distasteful.

Maybe it is different in other parts of the world. But in North America, I have seen "Christian" come to mean out-of-touch, ultra-conservative, angry, fake, and hypocrite. In the United States, a Christian is a Republican who lives in a nice neighborhood in a nice house and visits the poor on mission trips.

I'm sure I have just offended many readers who will stop reading now, put this book down, and write nasty letters to the publisher. If that's how they feel, I guess it's probably best that they stop reading now. But in case you haven't set the book down already, realize that I'm not trying to make this up.[2] It may be from personal experience, but I feel as if Christianity has become more identified with politics and issues that we stand for (or against) than it is identified with following and becoming like Jesus Christ. Not that these things can't be a part of what it means to follow Jesus, but what bothers me is that we have made it *the* identity and *the* way to follow Jesus. In some way, we have it backward.

We live in a North American culture where Christianity has been the predominant religion for many years. A Christian culture—a Christian way of doing life has developed. And over time, it has become distorted. We start identifying the faith with the culture until the one has replaced the other. Instead of the faith shaping the culture, the culture has shaped the faith. So now, being a Christian has come to mean one thing—one way of following that has been immersed in, filtered through, and distorted by our culture's values. The result is that we have a consumer mindset, an entertainment-

obssessed, materialistic, reactionary way of following Jesus. It is very different from a way of following Jesus without that cultural distortion.

Now, realize that we can't do our faith in a vacuum—completely separate from culture. That is impossible. We can't eliminate culture—we exist within culture. (Culture is the way we do life—we all need to eat, but the way we prepare food, what spices we use, whether we use forks or chopsticks—that is a part of culture. It would be silly to try to remove all that and eat raw food with our hands off the floor. That is not what I'm trying to say.) All religion exists in culture. However, "The continuing challenge of Christianity is to live in the kingdom of God within our particular time and culture, without letting the culture overpower the kingdom."[3] I would contend the challenge is living out the kingdom without creating a false Christianity—and thinking that we are influencing our culture, when it is actually the other way around.

LOSING THE WAY

I don't mean to sound bitter. Honestly, it just makes me sad. I keep wondering how this happened. I want to use a different term, a different word to identify my faith. A long time ago, followers of Jesus were known as that—they were called "followers of the Way." Maybe that would work better. I don't know. All I know is that . . .

At some point, we lost something.

I want to go back. I want to go back to a day when Christianity meant something more—when it meant something honorable, and it was not something to be embarrassed about. When you said the name "Christian," people knew what kind of person you were and that realization made them feel safe, comforted, at peace, and at times convicted by the Holy Spirit. Maybe when they heard the word, they might even smile.

Could it be that we have put on so many layers of our own culturally-corroded, sin-veined, suburban-selfishness flavored, bland brand of Christianity that we can't recognize the real thing anymore? Is it possible that we have molded Jesus into our own image (instead of the other way around) to the point that we don't recognize him in our lives anymore? Is it possible that the image of him is so distorted and disfigured that when we actually try to share Christ with our friends and families, he is rejected? Is it possible that his twisted visage is only a horrible Dorian Gray portrait,[4] and not a true representation of the real, eternal, living Son of God?

Every year my family buys me one of those daily tear-off-page calendars that sit on your desk. I always get the one with words on it. It is like a daily dictionary. I tear off and save my favorites. One recent word of the day was *soi-disant* (pronounced, "swah disahhn." You can say it with a snooty French accent for effect, if you like). The word means, "so-called, or self-styled."[5] It means we define something for ourselves. If someone was bragging, they might call themselves a "great leader," and if you disagreed with them, you might say, "Yeah right, more like a *soi-disant* leader" (meaning "in your own mind, by your own definition, you are a great leader").

SOI-DISANT BELIEF

I think that term describes it well; *soi-disant*—self-labeled, self-created, self-believed. "So called." I think it applies here. What we have created is a *soi-disant* Christianity. A Christianity defined by self. We have changed the word "Christian" to represent a religion we have created to suit our desires. It is something of our own devices, to meet our own needs. We have put layer upon layer of Christian culture (Christianese) and self-serving interests on top of it. We have buried Jesus so far underneath our trappings that we could completely live out this *soi-disant* religion without ever really believing in or surrendering[6] to the real, living, New Testament Christ.

I used to like Christian music (not the "everything sounds the same Nashville cookie cutter radio play" stuff, but the real creative cutting edge or real spirit of worship stuff). Sometimes the good music can be hard to find, so I would spend hours listening at a Christian book store. One time, I thought I had found an album worth trying, so I got in line to make my purchase. In line ahead of me was another shopper, a well-dressed woman who was holding a small dog in her arms.

I don't know what kind of dog it was, but it had all of its fur pulled into little tufts, rubber-banded together. So there were dozens of fur poofs jotting out, all with small, twisted rubber bands at their base. It must have taken hours to pull all that fur into little tufts like that.

The lady behind the counter noticed it too, and made a comment. "What a beautiful dog!"

The woman made no hesitation. "Yes it is," she proudly declared. "The dog's name is 'Honor.' You see, we asked God for a championship show dog, and God gave us this dog. God *honored* his promise to us. Honor has won several dog show competitions, and is one of the best show dogs in her category." Both the store clerk and I smiled for a moment, a bit caught off guard by her enthusiasm.

Now I don't know if it was the setting (surrounded by the stuff of our consumer Christian culture—right there at the checkout were "Testamints," breath mints with crosses on them—I mean, seriously . . .), and I don't know why it hit me the way it did. I love dogs; I grew up with dogs in the house my entire life. I don't have anything against dogs. But something was bothering me. By the time I got to my car, the weight of that moment hit me.

SHOW DOGS???

Is that the best understanding we have of the kingdom of God—show dogs? That is what we pray for, and trust God for? Is that what our Christian faith has become? Is that what Jesus desired and hoped for us when he died on the Cross? Show dogs?

I am not trying to purposely offend anyone, but maybe our idea of faith should be challenged at this point. When did Christianity become so turned upside down? When did it become about us? It just seems that Christianity has morphed into something it wasn't meant to be, and everyone just accepts it as the real thing. If I am being judgmental, I pray for your forgiveness and mercy. Seriously. I mean it. I don't want to judge, lest I be judged. Obviously, I can't know the heart or motives of someone in line ahead of me at the bookstore. However, it seems to me that when we have formed our lives around things that are very insignificant and have no eternal consequence whatsoever, we aren't very interested in following the will of God, or surrendering our lives to whatever God may desire to do with it. At that point, we are more interested in pursuing our own will and dreams (like our dreams of having a champion show dog) and taking God along for the ride. I mean seriously, on Judgment Day, is Jesus going to run up to this woman and say, "Am I glad that you prayed for that champion show dog—I was really afraid that Satan was going to steal another dog show championship away from the kingdom of God." Maybe I'm wrong, but that doesn't seem like following God in obedience, it seems like *leading* God on a leash and calling on him to give us what we want to make us happy. *Soi-disant.*

OK. I'm sorry. I guess I'm being too hard on this lady (by the way, if you happen to know her, or you see any lady with a rubber-banded fur dog in a Christian bookstore, you might recommend that she not buy this book).[7] I am being too hard on her—because I know I'm no different. I've bought into the same layered, buried, personal consumer kingdom faith. I would prefer that God cater to my whims instead of me surrendering to being a follower of the Way. Maybe the only difference between me and the dog lady is that somehow, deep down, I feel that I've lost something—I'm missing something. It aches inside me. Maybe that lady thinks a dog-centered Christian life is what it is supposed to be. I don't. I *know* I've turned Christianity into something that allows me to live unchanged, and live for myself, and it is tearing me up inside. When I compare that life to what I read in the Bible, I know that my life and the life depicted there are not the same. And when I start being honest with myself, and look at the glimpses of Jesus we have in the New Testament, and compare them to what I *think* I know of him—it makes me sad.

 When did God change from the great giver of life to a MasterCard for our selfishness?

What if I have been living out my so-called Christian life, and I have got it all wrong?

WOULD WE KNOW IF IT WAS WRONG?

Think about this for a minute. What if everything you have heard, know, and understand about Christianity—is wrong? Is it possible? Could it be that we have so distorted the faith that most of what we believe and know about it is completely off base? Oh sure, there are some cracks in the cover-up where the light gleams through, there are moments and glimpses of truth, but for the most part, is it possible that we have misunderstood, misinterpreted, and undone much that Jesus did and taught?

Now, for those of you who disagree with me on that point, consider this. It may be possible that we are so far gone, our understanding is so distorted, that we don't even realize it. When someone would speak the truth to us, we would think they were lying or exaggerating. But we have to open our minds to the possibility that we don't understand Jesus and the Way to follow him. We must consider the possibility that we have been following a way that is so distorted *and so widely accepted* that everyone around us believes it, so that the distorted picture seems like the real thing.

Don't think that is possible? This is exactly the situation during the time when Jesus walked the earth. There was a religion (the Jewish religion) that had gotten so far from what it was supposed to be about that much of Jesus' recorded ministry is spent arguing with their religious leaders and turning their idea of following God on its head.

Don't believe me? Let's take a closer look at an example from the Bible. Let's start with the Sermon on the Mount, found in Matthew 5—7.

JESUS AND THE LAW

Some quick background—Jesus is talking to a Jewish audience. The Jewish people were those who believed in God and followed God's law based on what had been revealed to them in the Old Testament. Jesus starts walking his hearers through the "Law of God," but what he says about it is not what they know. In fact, it is so different from their understanding that he starts with a disclaimer! What he is about to say is so different from what they understand to be the truth that he has to tell them ahead of time that he knows and believes that this is the law of God—God's holy word passed down to them. He is about to tell them truth that has been so hidden underneath their religious understanding that it is going to sound wrong to them—so he reminds them that he really does think the law of God is important, and that he affirms and respects it.

He affirms the law with a spoonful of sugar to help them swallow the medicine of truth. "Do not think that I have come to abolish the Law or the Prophets; I have not come to abolish them but to fulfill them. I tell you the truth, until heaven and earth disappear, not the smallest letter, not the least stroke of a pen, will by any means disappear from the Law until everything is accomplished. Anyone who breaks one of the least of these commandments and teaches others to do the same will be called least in the kingdom of heaven, but whoever practices and teaches these commands will be called great in the kingdom of heaven" (Matthew 5:17-19). Did you catch that? What he is about to say next is not abolishing the law, but *fulfilling* it.

Then comes the sucker punch, the slap in the face that they were not expecting: "For I tell you that unless your righteousness surpasses that of the Pharisees and the teachers of the law, you will certainly not enter the kingdom of heaven" (Matthew 5:20). What? We have it wrong? What we have been taught is not the real thing—not a true understanding of righteousness? You mean the way we have been following is not the real way? Not enter the kingdom? He must be kidding . . .

But he is not kidding. Jesus goes on to explain. "You have heard that it was said to the people long ago, 'Do not murder, and anyone who murders will be subject to judgment.' But I tell you . . ." (Matthew 5:21-22a). OK, we have to slow down here or we will miss it. Let's break this down. "You have heard that it was said . . ." What was said? "Do not murder." But where does that come from? Who said it? It is a direct quote from the Old Testament, from the law of God—actually from the TEN COMMANDMENTS. OK, so it is a direct quote from God himself. Written by the finger of God on some stone tablets and given to Moses, and passed on to the Israelites, the Jewish people—God's chosen ones.

Then Jesus does something very interesting. He makes a correction. "But I say . . ."

We have just said that Jesus did not come to abolish the law, but to fulfill it. He is not making a correction in the TEN COMMANDMENTS, is he? Why would he make such a sharp contrast? Jesus makes this contrast because even though he is quoting the law of God, that is not what the people are hearing. They had so buried the law of God under their interpretations, under their traditions, under their culturally influenced understanding of it, that they no longer *heard* the real thing. Jesus is not correcting the law, he is letting the people know that they have missed the real thing. They have created a way of doing the law that is not the real way. So Jesus is pointing them back to what it was intended to be.

Jesus then goes on to explain the meaning behind the law. It is about the heart. Truthfully, you can keep that commandment by staying in bed all day, and never going near anyone. But the intent of God's law is about more than murder as an act. Jesus says watch your words, and even if someone has something against you (whether or not you have something against them), go and repair the relationship. You see, this law is about love.

The religious leaders and Jewish people had made it about just barely keeping the law. "Don't murder" became carefully defined, including clarifying times when it might be acceptable to kill someone. Jesus cuts to the chase and explains the original intent—not figuring out when you should kill or not kill but instead, seeking love and actively finding the way to restore the relationship with those who hold a grudge against you.

Jesus keeps going, following the same pattern:
>You heard this (from God, but it has not been rightly understood)
>But I say (correcting the interpretation)
>The law is then correctly explained.

He does this with adultery, divorce, swearing, the "eye for an eye" principle, and what it means to love your neighbor. He also redefines giving, prayer, fasting, and what treasure is. The people and their leaders had so badly misinterpreted their religion that they thought as long as you don't touch the person, you can think whatever you want about them. So long as you didn't sin with your body, you could sin in your heart as much as you wanted. They thought that loving those who love you was enough, and that it was acceptable to hate those who hate you. But that is far from the heart of God, and if we want to be God's children, we must become like him and love even those who hate us. They thought that prayer and fasting were religious medals to be put on display, but that's not true when you follow in the way of Jesus. Following the practices of his way is more about living for God and not caring what other people think or trying to impress them.

Jesus walks them through this, not because the law of God was broken or should be rejected, but because it had been so misunderstood and twisted that it no longer reflected what it meant to follow God's way.

Are we like the people of that day? Do we desperately need Jesus to come and re-interpret and re-examine us to see if we are really following his way?

Could it be that the way of Jesus we are showing the world around us is not the real way?

Could it be that the world looks at Christians as strange, irrelevant, narrow-minded, and hypocritical, not *in spite* of how we have lived out our faith, but precisely *because of it*?[8]

WHAT'S MISSING

I think I know what the problem is. We have lost touch with something at the core of this way of believing and following. We are missing the most important ingredients. It is like leaving out an ingredient when baking a cake; it doesn't taste right. So if we back up and rewind to before a cake is a cake, we see it is a mix of separate ingredients that are each made up of other ingredients. A cake is made up of flour, eggs, and milk, and the flour, eggs, and milk are made out of building blocks (molecules, for you science types). If we go back far enough, we get to the elements—those primary core ingredients upon which everything else is built—which make up the ingredients that make up the mix that makes up the cake.

That is what is missing.

14

We are not just missing key ingredients, we are missing elements. The core of the core. The main ingredient of the main ingredient. You know if you break us down, we human beings are composed of elements. We are made up of the same elemental compounds as everything else. We are gas and metal and mostly water. And if we were missing one of those key elements, we would not have life.

But I'm not trying to talk about chemistry here. I'm trying to talk about life. Living. Spirit.

We are missing spiritual elements. And we are dying.

Chapter Two

WATER FIRE WIND

I imagine if you have read this far, you read the title of this book. It describes three elemental forces[9] in the natural world that represent forces of God—spiritual forces. Now I'm not trying to get all mystical here. I'm just trying to say that we are missing things, foundational things, core things, central things. Aspects of the spiritual life that we have forgotten or left behind, and it has crushed us.

The main thing is to keep the main thing the main thing[10]—if that is so, then we have failed as a religion. The main thing is no longer our main thing. A cultural Christian understanding of the faith has replaced the real thing. The imitation faith has left us dying of thirst, freezing cold, and breathless. It just won't do anymore.

THE KEY QUESTIONS

So what do we do now? If we decide that we can no longer live under the value system of a self-invented, self-serving faith, what do we do?

We have to return to the elements of the faith—an elemental way of following.

It seems to me that some have tried and rejected Christianity—but what they have rejected is not the real thing. They have tried our re-invented version of it, and did not find it to have any power for their lives. It is as if we have introduced them to an impostor Jesus, and they reject him because they sense that he is not genuine—and they are right. They have rightly rejected a false religion! We try the cardboard cut-out Christ, and we struggle with sin, put on a good face at church, and thirst for something more. Our friends find nothing appealing—it is an empty-calorie, potato chip faith with no nutrition. It tastes good for a time, but in the long run it leaves us weak and flabby.

But if our faith isn't missing key elements (the real nutritional ingredients), we might be able to introduce the world to the eternal, living Christ—the real one—and perhaps they would have their thirst quenched, find warmth, and discover their purpose for living.

But I am getting ahead of myself. Before we do that, we must ask ourselves a few key questions. These are questions that are foundational—the kind of questions that we didn't even know we were asking deep down in our heart of hearts. These questions will help us realize how far we have come, and will help us recognize the key ingredients that are missing from our lives. By raising these questions, we will be able to see if we have moved away from the original faith (and if so, how far we have moved away). Maybe you have already been asking these and trying to answer them for yourself. For the purposes of this book, I offer three key questions:

What is the way of Jesus?
What is the best life?
What does it mean to follow?

As human beings, we would want to know what is the best way to live out our lives. We are confronted by this Jesus who existed in history, and who presented a way of living. So we ask the questions, *what exactly is his way, is his way the best, and how does his way work?*

It is these three questions that we will try to answer in the rest of this book.

RETURNING TO THE ELEMENTS

Of course, we can never answer these questions if we are going the wrong way, or if we are examining some weak imitation of the real way. If the way is distorted, then our answers will be too. We will never know if following in the way of Jesus is the best way of living if we are following a different way that is of our own creation (or has been re-created by the values of the world). The problem has been that our misunderstanding of the way of Jesus goes so deep that we are like the Pharisees. We think we are doing it right, but what we think we know has become so twisted, and our understanding is so re-shaped, that we don't even realize that we have completely missed it. The Pharisees thought they had it right. Several times in the New Testament, they *corrected* Jesus because his new ways, practices, and interpretations of the faith were counter to their understanding. They were certain that they knew how to live their religion correctly. Much of the interaction between Jesus and the Pharisees shows Jesus explaining the correct interpretation of the law, and pointing out how badly they had missed the point.[11]

Unless we are content with missing the point too, it is important to make sure we are following in the true way. This is the only way we can be sure that our own interpretations and opinions on what it means to be a Christian have not been clouded and fogged up—only then will we know when we have lost our way.

THE WAY OF JESUS

The way of Jesus is about the story—not the verse. It is not merely a New Testament rule of living—it is the whole epic, Genesis to Revelation, water to water, ocean of chaos to river of life. Pillar of fire to lake of fire. Spirit hovering over the waters in Genesis to the violent wind from heaven in Acts.

The way of Jesus is about the question, not the easy answer. For far too long, Christianity has tried to make the way about having easy answers for any question—and it has never been that. Do you really think that we can understand, know, and communicate the God of the universe in a few simple answers? The way of Jesus is elemental, dynamic, and mysterious. It cannot be quantified. It is not too easily applied to life like a patch. It is the whole garment. It is woven into us.

We probably shouldn't try to hand it off to our friends with one sentence, like a pharmaceutical pill, "Just accept Jesus as your personal Savior," or

"Just pray about it," or proclaim "Jesus is the answer" (what was the question?). When we try to make it like that, we end up like the friends of Job—ready with answers, but not very helpful. The way of Jesus is something more than the miniature toy we make of it.

MINIMALIZED FAITH

Haven't we made it that? We have struggled to make our faith relevant to the world, and in the process we have minimalized it, shrunk it, until it no longer resembles the actual reality. We have tossed the world a tiny figurine of Jesus to place on their dashboard. We have handed them a small pamphlet (quite literally, in many cases) and have walked away expecting them to know all they need to know, and we think we have given them the answer. But all you get from a tiny pamphlet is a tiny god.

The result of this is that we have made knowing Christ about "just this" or "just that." Look a couple of paragraphs back. "*Just* accept Jesus as your personal Savior." You see? That is all you have to do. It is *just* about that. That is all there is to being a Christian, and really that is the point of it all, right? You *just*, or in other words, you minimally, simply, *only* have to accept him as Savior—that's all. Then you get to go to heaven, and the rest of us can relax about the uncomfortable task God has made us perform of trying to get you there. So *just* do it and then you can relax and so can we.

I believe that the way of Jesus is a little more complex than that, and a lot more mysterious.

Now, there is a difference between shrinking our faith and returning to the elements of our faith. Exploring the elements is not minimalizing—we are trying to get back to the genuine article, as simple or as complex as it may be. We are going back to the beginning, removing all the stick figure drawings and all of the complex, detailed blueprints and manuals, as well. We look at the thing in its purity—in its elemental form, before we changed it into something else.

THE THREE ELEMENTS

That is what is so beautiful about these elements. They are the original, genuine article. They are the parts of life out of which everything else is made and sustained. They are difficult to distort. We have a basic understanding of what they are supposed to be. Imitations and additives are easily spotted. We can easily tell when they are present, and when they are absent.[12]

So we have distilled all of discipleship down to three simple questions, three simple elements. Discipleship is not supposed to be about the latest program or the latest book (not even this one). It should be simple enough for a child to do. If all the law and the Prophets can be reduced to "love God and love your neighbor" (Luke 10:27, author's paraphrase), then perhaps the complexities of the Christian life can be expressed with three simple (undistorted) elements. In particular, we would do well to focus our attention on three critical elements that we have otherwise missed or twisted beyond recognition. If we could recapture these core ideas, then we could recapture a way of living that was joyful, powerful, and effective. If we were to live these elements, we may find a deeper sense of fulfillment in our lives. Perhaps we would represent Jesus to the world in a way the world has not seen in a long time.

When we talk about water, fire, and wind, what do we mean by them and what do they represent? These three elements represent three foundational aspects of the way of following Jesus that have been lost, changed, or distorted. They are vital to our spiritual lives. I will explain them here and on the rest of these pages. Simply put:

Water is grace.
Fire is holiness.
Wind is Spirit.

Let me put them in relation to the key questions we talked about earlier. These elements of following help us to understand how to better ask and answer the key questions about following in the way:

What is the way of Jesus? (Water)
What is the best life? (Fire)
What does it mean to follow? (Wind)

Water is what sustains life. Fire is the agent of change that transforms whatever it touches. Wind is the energy that moves over the whole earth.

Water represents the grace of God that sustains all life and faith. It is the way of Jesus, and the way we follow him. Fire represents the purity that comes when everything else has been burned away. Wind represents the movement of the Spirit of God over the whole earth, accomplishing his will. It is our invitation to join that movement.

Beautifully and simply, we must have these elements in our lives in order to follow in the way of Jesus. Without water, we die of thirst. Without fire, we are choked by cold impurities. Without wind, we are stagnant, still, and stale.

How is following in the way of Jesus the best life? When it has water, fire, and wind.

SECTION ONE
WATER ▽

GRACE LIKE WATER

Grace is a life-changing gift.

But once again, we don't get it. Some re-education is necessary. Instead of the idea of grace transforming us and the world around us, it has been suppressed. Grace has been relegated to the nostalgic feeling we get when we sing "Amazing Grace." And that is about the only time we talk about it. Our minds have been warped by our culture, and we have a difficult time accepting grace as real—let alone allowing it to shape all that surrounds us. But this is powerful stuff. The floodwaters of this idea can change the course of our lives.

WATER

We live by water. It is the largest element in our bodies (we are about 50 percent water), and we would not survive one week without it.[13] Early civilizations developed around rivers where there was water available to drink.

It is difficult to imagine today in North America how dependent we are on water. For us, we turn on a faucet, and it's there. We take it for granted. It is a given. We don't think and act like civilizations before us who looked to God and prayed for water.

For them, water was not a given. They were very aware of their dependency on it. If the heavens stopped bringing water and there was a drought, people would die.[14]

I remember traveling in Uganda. I went to a remote village to visit a church school. As soon as I arrived, one of the children took me by the hand and ran with me down a path. It was the first thing he wanted to show me. It was the water well, complete with a hand crank pump. He stood back and smiled. He was so proud of it. I learned that not every village had one. This access to water meant the village was sustainable and could survive. This little boy understood a very important concept—water meant life.

We rely on water, but consider this—we don't *deserve* water. Yes, I know we just said that we must have water to survive. But that doesn't mean we have earned it or deserve it. Think of it like this. Water falls free from the sky. It waters the earth and makes way for life to happen. It is something God has built into the planet to sustain life. It was here, set in place before you ever arrived, and it will be here making life possible after you are gone. It is free. It is part of the weather system on earth, and God is free to withhold it or make it pour. It falls free to the earth on those who are good and those who are evil. Did you catch that? That is the link between water and grace.

Grace has been there all along seeping through the pages of the Bible, but we didn't really catch it or notice it, and we just kept on reading. I'm going to walk through a couple of passages to help us understand it. But first, we have to strip away all that we think we know, and then we have to come to grips with just how misunderstood, how very different this idea is—and how powerful and transforming it is.

MISUNDERSTOOD GRACE— COUNTER TO ALL WE KNOW

As I have said above, one of the problems is that we have let our surrounding culture influence our faith. And like so much of our faith, we have minimalized the power of this idea. We have made one of the most significant gifts of God small. We have squeezed the bigness of it into a plastic bottle with a label and a marketable name. We haven't taken the time to understand it, so our definitions shrink it. Grace has become G.R.A.C.E.—"God's Riches At Christ's Expense." That is a nice idea, and a happy thought, but that doesn't begin to capture the depth of the meaning of grace.

It is so easy to miss grace. I was a Christian for fifteen years and I never caught it. Grace is nearly the opposite of what we see all around us. It is counter to most of what we have been taught and have accepted as the way life works. At times, there is something within us that resists it.

We have spent most of our lives being hurt and broken, so we have had to fight back with "an eye for an eye" mentality. We have been hurt so much that we feel we must hurt others back, just to see the scales balanced. We have seen so many criminals let off the hook and get away with murder that when we finally catch one, we want to see them get the penalty for their actions—because that is what should happen. Our "law and order" society, combined with our own hurts (or times when true fairness has been harshly enacted upon us), work together to distort our view until we think that being offered grace or offering grace would somehow be criminal.

Because grace is different from the way the world works, it takes a while for us to understand it. Then it takes even longer to realize that God meant for us to live by it.

REDEFINING THE WORD

I was studying all about God in seminary. One day a professor read three paragraphs that taught me more about God and his ways than I learned in the rest of the three and a half years I spent there. It was a definition of grace that I will share with you now. I am about to pass along a gift to you, so I ask you, please, please don't miss this.

There is no way I can define grace better than has already been written in the masterful words of Frederick Buechner (pronounced "Beekner"), so I will quote him here. Apart from the words of the Bible itself, these words have transformed my life more than any other. I offer them here to be a foundation of our discussion, but also for you to savor. Read this definition of grace slowly and deliberately, like letting chocolate melt on your tongue, for the pure enjoyment of it, for this is grace:

> Grace is something you can never get, but can only be given. There's no way you can earn it or deserve it or bring it about anymore than you can deserve the taste of raspberries and cream, or earn good looks or bring about your own birth.

A good sleep is grace and so are good dreams. Most tears are grace. The smell of rain is grace. Somebody loving you is grace. Loving somebody is grace. Have you ever *tried* to love somebody?

A crucial eccentricity of the Christian faith is the assertion that people are saved by grace. There is nothing *you* have to do. There is nothing you *have* to do. There is nothing you have to *do*.[15]

When I heard those words, suddenly, I got it. Well, at least I started to get it. I had heard about grace before, but it was so different from all that I knew that I missed it. Then I heard those words and for the first time it sank in—there was nothing I had to do. I had been given a great gift, and that gift was the love and grace of God.

God loved me and there was nothing I had to do—nothing I could do to make him love me more or less. I couldn't make him love me more by being good and I couldn't make him love me less by being bad. I am loved by the one who is love. I am loved beyond my ability to comprehend, and that is grace, and that is the point. God's love is grace because it is given freely to us without expecting anything in return. I don't have to work to earn God's love. I don't have to balance the scales. I am loved. Period.

So grace is the gift of all God's free love and free provision and free kindness and blessing—without having to do anything beforehand to get it, and without having to do anything afterward to pay it back. God actively pours love and goodness and blessing into your life—pursuing the best for you, always and only. There is nothing you have to do.

It sort of surprised me that it was so simple. Why didn't I get it before? I began to realize that if we misunderstood grace, it would have an effect on the way we read our Bibles. And then we risk making the mistake of reading something into our Bibles that isn't there. Or the opposite, we miss something that *is* there. I began to wonder where was grace in the Bible, and how had I missed it?

THE RAIN OF GRACE

I had read through the New Testament several times and never saw it there, right there in those pages. I want to walk through some of these biblical examples of grace because I don't want you to miss this. Grace is so foundational to our lives (and the rest of this book) but it takes time to grasp. One of the key Bible passages where grace is hidden is from the Sermon on the Mount in Matthew 5:

> You have heard that it was said, 'Love your neighbor and hate your enemy.' But I tell you: Love your enemies and pray for those who persecute you, that you may be children of your Father in heaven. He causes his sun to rise on the evil and the good, and sends rain on the righteous and the unrighteous. If you love those who love you, what reward will you get? Are not even the tax collectors doing that? And if you greet only your own people, what are you doing more than others? Do not even pagans do that? Be perfect, therefore, as your heavenly Father is perfect (vv. 43-48, TNIV).

Once again, Jesus must correct the understanding of the day. He quotes the law in Leviticus (19:18), "Love your neighbor." The next part of the quote, "hate your enemy," was an addition by the teachers and the people themselves. It is a non-grace understanding of love, an "eye for an eye" balancing of the scales. Love your neighbor, but not your enemy—feel free to treat them as they have treated you. Pay them back with whatever hate, harm, and revenge you can muster for how they have treated you.

But Jesus goes on to fix what they have distorted. He explains that the whole reason behind the command to love others is based not on human understanding, but on God's love. God wants us to love like he does. And how does God love? God loves with grace.

The example he gives is sunlight and rain. God sends life-giving sunlight and water upon both the good and the bad. He doesn't just water the gardens of the good, leaving the ones who choose evil to starve in a cropless desert dustbowl. He offers them love and goodness, regardless of how they respond to him. The people of the earth could hate God, curse him, and worship Satan—and God would offer them a cup of cold water to quench their thirst. He would love them no matter what their response, and sometimes in spite of it.

This is the point of the passage. Love generously and inclusively without regard to what you will get in return, for this is the way that God loves. Rain falls on the just and unjust—by grace. Grace falls like water on us every day as God moves in our midst to act on our behalf, whether we even realize it or not. Grace like water.

The book of Joel in the Old Testament makes the same connection of water to grace. God's people have drifted from his ways and they are facing famine. Locusts have eaten up all the food, and people and animals are going to starve. Through the prophet, God says to his people that instead of mourning they should turn back to God—"Give me your hearts," he says. God tells them they can come back to him and he won't punish them for their wrongs—and that he will restore their crops by sending rain. "Rejoice in the LORD your God! *For the rains he sends are an expression of his grace*" (Joel 2:23, NLT,[16] emphasis added).

THE GENEROUS LANDOWNER

I don't want to go on and on about this, but it took me so long to get it that I think another couple of examples will help. Another explanation of grace is found in Matthew 20:1-16. Without putting the whole passage here, let me retell it quickly.

There is a landowner who goes to hire some workers. He finds some on the street corner at the beginning of the day. He agrees to pay them a day's wage to work the full day and gets them out to his vineyard to work. Then he goes back later, at 9 A.M., noon, and 3 P.M. and hires more workers each time. Then he goes back at about 5 P.M., an hour before quitting time, and finds some more workers sitting around doing nothing. So he gets them out to his vineyard to work about an hour before it gets dark.

At the end of the day, when the landowner goes to pay them, he starts with the ones he hired last, the ones who worked only an hour or so at the end of the day. He pays them a full day's wage! So at the back of the line, the ones he hired first, who have worked all day, who have toiled through the heat of midday, and worked more than anyone else—they start getting excited because they figure if those workers hired at the end of the day get a full day's pay, the ones who actually worked a full day will get paid more.

But when they get up to the table, the landowner gives them a full day's pay—exactly what they agreed to work for. That's all. And they are upset.

And they should be upset (and we are sometimes upset that this is in the Bible). Those workers got cheated. They feel they were not treated equally. And you know what? They are right—they weren't. Their way of thinking makes sense.

But this is grace. This is why grace is counter to everything we know. This parable doesn't make any sense until we realize that grace is not fair. It is not fair. It is grace. The point of the story is not to affirm all that we believe about being treated equally. This is a story about the *grace and generosity of the landowner*.

The workers who worked a full day didn't really get cheated—they agreed to work a full day for a full day's pay, and that is exactly what they got. They were treated fairly. However, this landowner treated others *more than fairly*—they were given grace. Instead of getting upset that some got exactly what they bargained for, we should be celebrating the generosity of this person who gave others *more* than they bargained for.

The only thing that helps this story make sense in our minds is grace. The whole point of the story is to show us that God, in his generosity and love, gives freely to us—*whether or not we have earned it*. It is not fair; it doesn't make sense in this world, and that is the point.

29

In some ways, I think this story is God's way of trying to prepare the church to get used to the fact that when we all get to heaven, we are going to be a bit surprised. There will be some there who were Christians all of their lives, surrendered their lives as missionaries, and never missed a Sunday in church. And to their surprise, standing right next to them will be a cigarette-breathing child pornographer who in fear turned to trust Christ on their deathbed—*and received the same grace*. Isn't this what Jesus was talking about when he re-educated the religious ones of his day, saying, "the tax collectors and the prostitutes are entering the kingdom of God ahead of you" (Matthew 21:31)?

And on that day we won't be able to talk about fairness, but perhaps we will finally know what we meant all those years by *amazing* grace.

THE CANCELED DEBT

If we haven't caught it yet, perhaps one more look in Matthew will help us understand how the Bible explains grace. Matthew 18:21-35 has another story that oozes grace, but we don't always catch it; instead we read right past it.

In this passage, the question is forgiveness. Jesus tells an illustration of a king settling debts with his servants. One servant has borrowed too much and owes the equivalent of millions of dollars. The king orders that his family be sold into slavery to pay the debt. The man begs for more time. The passage says that the king "took pity on him" (v. 27) and cancelled the debt. It is an incredible act of generosity that should be celebrated.

But apparently, the servant hasn't learned the lesson. He goes out and instead of celebrating, instead of passing on that same grace, he withholds it. The servant runs into a friend who borrowed the equivalent of about twenty bucks. He demands it back and tries to choke it out of him. Word of this gets back to the king. Essentially, the king says, "OK, if you want your friend to live by the 'law' (and without grace), then so will you. You want to live without grace, you got it." Then the servant whose debt was cancelled is thrown into prison until the debt is paid.

Now when we read this story, or when we hear it taught, we often quickly move to the moral at the end, "This is how my heavenly Father will treat each of you unless you forgive a brother or sister from your heart" (v. 35, TNIV). So the lesson we learn is that we should forgive our brothers and sisters. Yes, that is the moral of the story. But don't miss the grace in those pages—the foundation underneath this story is God's grace. Yes, we should forgive those around us—but don't miss the heart of the matter. We *have first been forgiven a huge debt, for no reason except God's loving grace.*

We want things to make sense, and the way we make sense of the story is to say, "We should forgive others or we won't be forgiven." We like the nice, neat balance of those scales because it helps this story make sense in our minds. (Could it be that we like the "policeman" picture of God, pointing a finger at us and yelling, "I won't forgive you if you don't forgive, so watch out!" And that's the way we interpret it, isn't it?) But when we arrive at that conclusion too quickly, we miss a major point of this story—that God freely, for no reason but love and grace, has forgiven us. So the real point of the story is not to make a nice legal exchange, like buying grace at the grace store or forgiving *first* to be forgiven. The real point is that we have been freely *forgiven first*, and that is grace. Then, if we want to love like God, we will love freely, because we have become full of grace and are becoming like him. We are forgiven for no reason except grace—we love like God when we forgive others the same way.

THE ADULTEROUS WOMAN

Jesus not only talked about grace, he lived it out. There is one story of this that has captivated my attention for years. It is the story of the woman caught in the act of adultery, found in John 8:1-11:

> Jesus went to the Mount of Olives.
>
> At dawn he appeared again in the temple courts, where all the people gathered around him, and he sat down to teach them. The teachers of the law and the Pharisees brought in a woman caught in adultery. They made her stand before the group and said to Jesus, "Teacher, this woman was caught in the act of adultery. In the law Moses commanded us to stone such women. Now what do you say?" They were using this question as a trap, in order to have a basis for accusing him.
>
> But Jesus bent down and started to write on the ground with his finger. When they kept on questioning him, he straightened up and said to them, "Let any one of you who is without sin be the first to throw a stone at her." Again he stooped down and wrote on the ground.
>
> At this, those who heard began to go away one at a time, the older ones first, until only Jesus was left, with the woman still standing there. Jesus straightened up and asked her, "Woman, where are they? Has no one condemned you?"
>
> "No one, sir," she said.
>
> "Then neither do I condemn you," Jesus declared. "Go now and leave your life of sin" (TNIV).

OK, there is much happening in this passage: the teachers and Pharisees are trying to trap Jesus in his words, and they have caught a woman in adultery. (Where is the man? It takes two to tango, why don't they bring him too?)

Take a close look at how Jesus handles this question about the law. The Pharisees and teachers correctly explain the punishment laid out in the law: the woman should be stoned to death. The question they ask is, "In the Law Moses commanded us to stone such women. Now what do you say?" (v. 5). Their concern is the law of God. I imagine that they want to see if Jesus will uphold the law. I suspect that they probably feel that Jesus has not upheld the law in the past (look back to the words of Jesus we just explored; the religious authorities feel that his stance on grace is a threat to the law).[17] I fully expect that these teachers plan to stone this woman to death. The trap they are setting for him is that they expect him to say "No—don't stone her." Then they can discredit Jesus as a false teacher, because he would not have been teaching people to obey the law of God given to Moses.

Jesus resists the trap by not answering; instead he writes in the sand. In another act of grace, he is giving the teachers a chance to reconsider and back off. Jesus knows that the only difference between these teachers of the law and this woman is that the woman's sins are exposed. ("The Pharisees were correct when they said that adulterers and adulteresses were to be killed [Lev. 20:10; Deut. 22:22] but tragically mistaken when they assumed that they, as secret sinners, were qualified to render the capital punishment.")[18]

So, Jesus does not directly answer their question. Instead, he points out their false motives and hidden sins, reminding them that they are in no position to judge this woman. He redirects the question back at them, saying, "Let any of you who is without sin be the first to throw a stone at her" (v. 7). Jesus essentially says, "OK, you want to enforce the law of God? Fine. But if we are going to do it, realize that you have to include yourselves. The only ones who shouldn't be stoned to death for their sins are the ones who have no sin—so they can go first and throw the first rock." (By saying it this way, Jesus escapes their trap. He does not say that God's law is invalid—he upholds the law; he only asks that it be applied properly.) And so they all drop their stones and walk away, realizing that Jesus is right, they are no different from this woman—they too deserve punishment under the law.

Now, don't miss the next part. Once they have all gone, Jesus gets up and addresses the woman. "Where are they? Has no one condemned you?" (v. 10). She says that no one has. Then Jesus replies, "Then neither do I" (v. 11).

Here is grace, my friends. The Bible tells us that Jesus is without sin—he is the only one who actually could honestly pick up the stones and throw them! He knows the law, and knows that this woman is guilty, and by the law, she should be stoned to death. Yet instead of going ahead and enforcing the law at this moment, he says a strange thing: "If none of the ones with sin are going to condemn you today, then neither will I, the one without sin, condemn you."

And then he lets her off the hook.

I realize that there will be some who will argue with me on this point. Some will say that I am out of my head and have gone off the deep end. But as I read it, this story is not just to show us that Jesus can cleverly escape a trap. Here is the way I read it. Jesus is confronted by a woman caught dead to rights in sin, who stands before him facing the penalty of death—and he lets her off the hook. He does not hold her sin against her, but excuses her, instructing her not to do that anymore. The only way to explain his actions is by grace.

Do you see what is at stake here? Either the law of God is valid and should be applied and the woman should be killed by Jesus on the spot. Or—the law of God is invalid, and we can throw out the whole Old Testament, and while we are at it, throw out the Jewish religion and Christianity too, for they are both based on it. Or—there is a third option. The third option is that the law is valid, and the woman deserves death (not at the hands of the conniving teachers of the law, but certainly she bears the guilt of her sin). At the same time the law is valid, Jesus, in his love, commutes her sentence—he sets her free. He says, "Although you have sinned, you are not condemned. And you don't have to ever be condemned—just leave this sin behind." This is an act of grace. Grace is the only thing that allows me to say that Jesus fulfils the law and still does the loving thing. Here, grace and justice are in perfect balance, and the woman is given a fresh start. The past has been forgiven and forgotten—a better way of life awaits her if she will leave her life of sin.

How we interpret this passage and the ones before it is vitally important. It affects the way we treat others as we follow in the way of Jesus. If we are not careful, we end up treating others the way the Pharisees and teachers of the law did. We put ourselves in the position to be "stone throwers," judging others for their sins and holding it over them. But as we see from this passage, that is not the way of Jesus.

THE WAY OF JESUS IS GRACE

Remember the key questions from the previous chapters? One of them was, "What is the way of Jesus?" (We want to know what that is so that we can follow it . . .) Here is a quick answer: *Grace* is the way of Jesus.

Let's go back to the passage in Matthew 5 just for a second, the one that talks about loving your enemies. Jesus invites us to live out grace—to do more than just love only those who love us. It is a normal human response, to make an even exchange and only give when we get. But Jesus says that God loves all, whether they are good to him or bad. So as God's children, made in God's image, and loved with God's love—we then love others freely and openly, even if they are our enemies. We do it because that is the way God does it. The way of Jesus is grace. What makes us like Jesus, Christ-like, is offering grace to others.

A friend of mine came to me because she was having problems with her boyfriend. He had said some mean things to her that had really hurt her. She kept rehearsing for me what she was going to say to him to get back at him. But as we talked, more and more we reflected on the life of Christ. It became apparent to us both that no matter how much pain she was in right now, it didn't justify her saying hurtful things in return. We considered to-gether the lesson of the one whose debt was canceled—we have first been forgiven a huge debt. We are living in a time of celebration, not vengeance. When my friend thought about it like that, it made her smile. She decided to change her plans, and to talk to her boyfriend about what he said—but not to return the hurt.

When we are hurt by someone, we don't return hurt for hurt,[19] but instead we offer grace when we are hurt. This is the way of Jesus.

Grace is supposed to flow like water. It should rain from our lives freely because we have received from God freely.

We can't really love until we have been loved by the one who is love.

We first receive grace, then we can in turn share God's grace with others. It is when we are filled with grace and know deeply that we are loved that we are able to care for those around us without using them to meet our own needs. It is when God has so filled our lives that we need nothing else—then we are free to love.[20]

Think about it. When Jesus was being nailed to a cross, how did he react? When they hurt him, put nails in his hands, and stabbed a spear into his side, what did he say? His response was, "Father forgive them, for they know not what they do" (Luke 23:34). Instead of returning hurt for hurt, he returned forgiveness for hurt. It is his way. And if we choose to follow him, it is our way.

THE PINE BY THE STREAM

In a far away land there was a great forest. The forest extended from the valley below all the way up to the tree line, high up on the mountainside, to a point so high that trees could grow no more. A little more than halfway up the mountain, in the middle of the forest, was a grove of pine trees.

These evergreens blanketed several acres. To the east of them there was a meadow of light green grasses, and to their west was a stream that ran down the mountain, carrying the melted snow from its highest peaks down into the lush valley. The pine grove hugged the edge of the rambling stream, clinging to its serpentine banks on one side and rolling over the landscape to the edge of the meadow on the other.

One young pine tree, about halfway grown, stretched its branches as high as it could to catch the sunlight from the midst of the older, taller trees. Some of the nearby trees moved some of their branches to the side so that the young pine could absorb the life-giving rays of the sun.

Fortunately, the young pine was rooted near the stream of water. It did not have to work hard or wait for the rains to get the water it needed to grow. The young pine extended one of its roots closer to the stream—it could feel itself growing taller by each sunrise, as the water coursed through its trunk and helped it grow. The other trees noticed the rapid growth of the young pine, and smiled—swaying in the wind to celebrate the life promise of the young tree. Seeing that it was planted close to the stream, they all knew that no drought could hinder its growth—and it would soon become one of the tallest pines in the grove.

All was green and good—the pines in the grove swayed daily with the wind, smiled with the sun, and grew deep roots. On the warm days, the sons and daughters of humankind would come to play in the grove. They would climb their branches and rest in their shade. It made the trees glad to serve the sons and daughters of humankind—to them it was a joy to share life with them and know that people truly enjoyed walking in these woods.

The young pine too took delight when the sons and daughters of humankind played in its branches. Because the young pine was not as tall as the others, it had branches closer to the ground, which made it easier for the smallest of humankind to climb. Several that year came to swing, climb, and find shade under the young tree.

On other days, just before sunrise, when the forest was mostly quiet, except for the chirping of a few early birds, the central sound was the splashing and rushing of the stream to the west. On these days, the young pine would look to the stream, and watch the flashing of its waters as it heard them applaud their way to the bottom.

One day, the young pine began to wonder about where the water came from. It leaned over as far as it could to look up the mountainside and see the source of the stream, but it could not. It could only see as far as the bend in the stream, where it curled around some rocks and vanished from sight. Curious as young ones often are, the young pine wondered aloud to the elder pines of the grove, "Where does the water come from?" (Of course, when I say that the pine wondered aloud, I mean that the pine spoke to the other pine trees the way that pines do—through the rustling of their needles and branches and by the movement of their bark. It would not have been audible to any human.)

"We don't know where it comes from, or why," barked one of the other pines.

One of the elder trees bent a branch in reply, "The water is almost as timeless as the Ancient One himself, little pine."

"But how did we come to find this stream and grow next to it?" returned the young one.

"You have it root-side up, little one. We did not come to be here by it. It came to be near us. And we grow where water rains and the stream flows. Without its steady stream, we would quickly brown and fade away. We are rooted here and cannot see that far to see where the water comes from, or how it moves from here to there. In times past, tree has talked to tree, and it came to us that the source of the water is from somewhere beyond, somewhere above the view of trees. We only know that it comes to us by stream and by cloud—we cannot see its source. We know not where the clouds come from that bring rain—only that the wind blows them here from far away. Even the tallest among us, the wisest and oldest one, cannot see the source of water. All we know is that it comes to us and gives us life and growth."

The young pine did not understand and was not satisfied with the answers from its older relatives. "But what did we do to make the stream bend toward us?"

The mature pines hushed themselves as the tallest among them spoke up. This tall tree was at the highest point of the grove and towered over the rest. It was as old as any other in this grove. It spoke slowly and majestically, even more majestic than normal tree-speak.

"We . . . did . . . nothing to bring the water. It . . . has . . . always been there for us. Too many seasons without it . . . and we dry up. This is the way of trees."

The young one knew better than to argue with the tallest of the pine trees.

Sunrise turned to sunrise, and days passed, and the young pine continued to grow. Every day it drew water from the stream, and every now and then it would rain—making everything fresh and green. It seemed to the young pine that the rain washed away the heaviness of the air and even cleaned the soil and somehow made it easier to grow. Day in and day out the water came and went—from who knows where, to who knows where. It was just there. There were the days of the visits from the sons and daughters of men and women, and there were the days of cloud and rain, and the days of sun.

The young pine grew quickly by the stream and soon was taller than many of the trees of the grove. It grew and grew—but one day, it stopped.

The young pine stretched its top branches as high as it could to make itself taller—but when it did, it felt pain in its trunk. So the tree leaned itself a bit to the side to look down at its own trunk.

The sight surprised and shocked the young tree. There around the base of its trunk were shelves of fungus. They were attached around and even under its bark, pulling nutrients out of the trunk of the tree. Further up its trunk was a patch of small holes. As the young pine watched, small insects crawled in and out of the holes that had been burrowed into its side. The young pine almost became ill to think about all of those insects crawling around inside of it, eating away and weakening its core.

The young pine then looked down at the ground, and noticed some of its roots had become exposed. (These were the roots on the side away from the stream). The roots that did not face the stream had not grown long and deep. Instead they were short and shallow. Some had come up out of the ground to catch the rain water before it ran down the mountain. So near the surface, they provided no anchor for the young pine. As it leaned over to see this sight, it suddenly noticed that it was not stable—it felt as if it was losing its balance and was going to fall over. The young pine quickly straightened itself so as not to fall. But as it stood straight, it could not help but wonder how long it would be able to stand with fungus and bugs and shallow roots.

Chapter Five

LIVING WATER

I have said that I can't live with the word "Christian" anymore, and much of that is because that term has come to represent a people who have not understood the element of grace.[21] In fact, I have started to subdivide Christians that I meet into two categories—those who live by grace, and those who don't.

There is a significant difference between the two. Those who don't live by grace tend to act in certain ways that are—well, not graceful. There is a generosity and hospitality of spirit that is absent. Without that, they tend to want to hold others to a strict standard of behavior. They themselves tend to act as if certain behaviors are the measures of our spirituality. Often, the focus is on specific do's and don'ts, by which we determine who is better and who is worse on some spiritual spectrum. I have observed that they often seem bitter that they have to live under all these rules, and they take that bitterness out on those who don't live by the rules. They seem uncomfortable around those who don't know Jesus. When they are around those who *do* know Jesus, they seem to be watching to see if other Christians are going to follow "the rules" or not.

43

GRACE VS. NON-GRACE

To these "non-grace Christians," grace is bound up by the law. It is not free. We have to do something to get it. So they go about living their lives, doing good for God for the sole purpose of trying to earn God's grace in return. Their model of grace is like a store where you buy things. *First you pay for it, then you get it.* To go into the store and walk out with something without paying for it is criminal. (And they have strict rules against that.)

On the other side of the coin, there are the "grace Christians." They live and operate from a different set of principles. They seem to understand that they are saved by grace alone and that their ability to perform won't win them any more favor from God. They are mindful of their reliance on God and are marked not by bitterness, but by gratefulness. They don't see themselves as any better or worse than anyone else; they are just thankful for all God has done for them. They are comfortable around those who don't believe in Jesus (because they know they are no better or worse, but that we are all in need of God). They are accepting of other Christians. They are not trying to live up to some standard, and so they don't put on a show. They would be willing to admit they struggle.

If we misunderstand grace, it affects every area of our lives. Here's how it works. Because we don't understand what grace is meant to be, we end up *withholding* it. We don't get it, so we don't live it and we don't extend it to each other. Let me give you an example.

I was working at a denominational headquarters running a short-term mission program. I had worked late one night, putting in an eleven-hour day. I had been working some long hours for several days in a row, and I was starting to wear down. The next day I was tired. I couldn't get out of bed. I made myself go to work, but by the time I got my lagging body up, I was running about an hour late. I was walking up the stairs to my office when I ran into a coworker from another department coming down the stairs. He looked at me and said, "You are late, work starts here at 8 A.M."

Now this was a Christian man in charge of a Christian program at a church headquarters. But what permeated his voice that day was law. The rules said work started at eight. He had to be there at eight, so anyone else who wasn't there on time was not following the rules and should be punished (or at least scolded on the stairwell). It did not matter that I had put in extra hours the previous day. (And I don't remember seeing him working late in the office that previous night . . .) There was no giving me the benefit of the doubt, no grace-filled question, "How are you? Are you tired? You must be working hard . . ." What would it have hurt to give me a word of encouragement instead of a lawful reminder? I knew I was late (and not without reason). I was tired and could have used some encouragement, or at least a kind word. But instead, I was reminded of the rules. Policy had become more important than people.

Now being confronted about being late one hour is not that big of a deal. And this man was not a mean or bad person. (I found out later that he often prayed for me!) But I remember that moment because it reinforced my subcategory. I knew that person was a Christian, but as I walked away that day, I thought to myself, "What happened to grace?" If we live as a non-grace Christian, we can still be Christian—but we withhold grace from others in small and big ways. We go on living by the law, requiring that those around us do the same. But I wanted grace to be more than that. I was worn out and I needed grace from God—and from my brothers and sisters in the faith. I saw it in the lives of some Christians, but not in others—and so I started to see them in terms of "grace Christians, or non-grace Christians."

LES MISÉRABLES

I am not the first to recognize the distinction between grace and non-grace people. The best way I can illustrate this idea is through the story of Les Misérables (pronounced "lay miz-er-ahb"). The two main characters represent these two divisions clearly.

Set in the French Revolution, a young man named Jean Valjean (pronounced "JHAHN val-JHAHN") becomes imprisoned for stealing bread to feed his family. During his time in prison, he is watched over and mistreated by a guard named Javert (pronounced "jhahvair"). Javert sees life in black and white and understands that these criminals are to be punished for what they have done wrong. To him, the circumstances do not matter—stealing bread to eat when you are starving deserves punishment just like stealing for greed.

Jean Valjean escapes from prison. On his way, he knocks on the door of a priest. The priest feeds him and invites him to stay the night. During the night, in an act of fear and desperation, Jean Valjean takes advantage of the situation. He steals the priest's silverware (made of real silver and quite valuable) and flees. He is quickly caught and lies to the police, saying that the priest "gave him the silverware." The police take him back to the house of the priest to check out the story.

We expect the priest to be angry for being robbed and having harm returned for his kindness. He should be mad. And Jean Valjean has been caught dead to rights—he now has no excuse. Where once he went to prison and perhaps did not deserve it, he certainly deserves to be punished for his actions. He is guilty, and his hard life should take a drastic turn for the worse. He will now have to face prison again, and cruel treatment at the hand of the guard Javert.

But here comes the twist to the story—it turns out that the priest is a "grace Christian." When the police drag in Jean Valjean and tell the priest his story, the priest agrees with it! He says that yes, of course he gave the silver to Jean Valjean—but that is not all. He tells the guards that he is surprised that Jean Valjean did not also take the silver candlesticks he offered! He has the candlesticks fetched and adds them to the stolen silverware in Jean Valjean's sack.

The priest then says, "You no longer belong to evil. . . . I've ransomed you from fear and hatred. And now I give you back to God."[22]

This single act of grace turns Jean Valjean from a man hardened by life's cruelty into a person marked by grace. He begins to live his life with the grace that was offered to him. He becomes mayor of a town, he takes care of a young lady who has been outcast and has nowhere to turn—he lives the rest of his life from a new perspective.

Javert lives a different life. He leaves the prison guard and begins to pursue Jean Valjean. He must make him pay for the rules that were broken. Even though Jean Valjean has been offered grace, Javert wants to make him pay for past debts. The scales must be balanced in his mind, and he relentlessly pursues the "criminal." He lives as one bound by the law. He doesn't understand grace, nor can he let anyone else live in its freedom. He is the perfect example of a "non-grace Christian." Even when grace is displayed right in front of his eyes, he can't see it. Even when he is touched by it, he can't offer it to anyone.

WITHHOLDING GRACE

When we don't understand grace, we don't accept it; when we don't accept it, we don't offer it. The result is that grace is withheld.

Sometimes we withhold grace in church, even without intending it. Through subtle actions and attitudes, we can create a place that is not grace-filled and accepting. Those who need help don't receive it, because they don't feel comfortable being themselves in church. They don't feel like they can really share from the heart or reveal their struggles because they don't see anyone else sharing that way. If our church life becomes focused on the "rules" and the behaviors our Christian culture says are acceptable, then those who don't yet follow those rules can feel intimidated. To them, church looks like a museum where good people come to be put on display. If you don't look like the perfect family or perfect Christian, you don't feel like you belong. If you have experiences from your past that don't match up with that image, you don't feel you can share it because everyone in the "museum" seems like they have it all together. We withhold grace when we let sin become a label and a separator between those who know God and those who don't. We withhold grace when we live without love and offer only judgment—when we put on a show and expect others to live up to Christian culture's external appearances, rather than feeling welcome and at peace in God's house.

That doesn't mean that we should stop being good people. But it does mean that we have to be very careful about having a grace-filled heart and not an attitude of superior self-righteousness. If we make church visitors or non-believers feel inferior because they aren't living by all the right behaviors, then we have withheld the grace that Jesus offers them. When we are good people but emphasize how we are living all the right behaviors, people who have never lived that way can feel like outsiders to the kingdom.

That is not the heart of Jesus that I read in the Bible. Jesus spent time with "sinners" and ate in their homes. He made them feel at home in his presence. Religious leaders criticized him because you weren't supposed to spend time with people who dressed like that, lived like that, or were a part of that crowd. Not if you were "righteous." But Jesus didn't care about that. Those who were un-churched and labeled "sinners" were his friends. In short, he loved them.

If we live like "non-grace" Christians, we end up treating people who are wounded or broken as if they should "pull themselves together" before they enter the church doors. And those who are already in the church and who feel wounded or broken—for them the expectation is that you can't be that—you have to keep up appearances. Broken, hurting, struggling, and suffering isn't the kind of image we put on display at the museum. You have got to have it all together. We seem to imply that if you are a Christian you can't be broken, so those who are hurting in the church have nowhere to go. We project this kind of atmosphere where we invite people to pray publicly at an altar in the front of the church, but no one wants to go—they are afraid. Afraid of what others might think. They don't feel comfortable being open about their relationship to God because they have not seen Christian examples of what it means to be open—to be full of grace. They feel embarrassed to admit faults and failings because we have shown them that the church is a place where you come to be on display when you have it all together. Heaven forbid they should get "caught" going to counseling or admitting that they struggle with sin. We have not provided them a safe place that sends the message, "you are loved and you will always be loved, by us and by God—no matter what." And when they don't feel that way in our midst, we know that we have withheld grace.

Isn't it possible that the church was meant to exist for those outside its walls? Shouldn't it be a place where those who have been beaten down by the world can come to seek God, be welcomed and accepted, and find safety and refuge? If not, then why do we call the big room where we meet to worship a "sanctuary"?

SHARING FAITH

Our view of grace is foundational. It will affect every area of our lives—from how we treat people on the stairwell, to how we respond to the homeless on the street or the sick halfway around the world. In particular, how we live out grace affects how we share our faith with those who do not yet know Jesus Christ. If we are "non-grace Christians," we will treat non-believers differently than if we are "grace Christians." Will we respond to the world around us like Javert or Jean Valjean?

What Jesus do we present to those outside church walls? Are we like the Pharisees and teachers of the law, bringing those we catch in sin to judgment? Are we so concerned that the world knows where we stand on "the issues" that they see us as opposed to them—an enemy and not a caring friend? Are we viewed as confrontational or loving? Do we show those around us anything different than how Christians are portrayed in the media? Do we interact with them at all?

I remember facing this as a teenager in our youth group. I showed up late for pizza night with my friend, Ben. The entire group of ten was crammed around one booth made for eight—eight in the booth and two standing at the end of the table. They made a nice little circle—but one was left out. One young man, who was a little older than the rest of the group, had been invited (forced) to come by his parents. He was sitting in the next booth over, by himself, smoking a cigarette.

Here was an interesting picture—an entire youth group crammed around one booth, and in the booth right next to them, one teenager (who obviously didn't know the rules of church—or the restaurant), right next to them—an outsider.

I was proud of my friend Ben, who took the lead. He walked over and paused for a moment looking back and forth at the two tables. Maybe it was because there was no room at the one, or maybe for other reasons . . . I don't know . . . but he turned and sat down with the lone young man. I followed Ben's lead and pushed him further in on the booth bench and sat down too. We asked the young man his name (Lincoln) and started to ask him what kinds of things he liked to do. He was into cars. Ben knew a little about cars, and I threw in what I knew about working on cars from driving my Honda Civic hatchback (in case you were wondering, a Honda Civic hatchback is not regarded on the same level as the Ford Mustang and Chevy Corvette—Lincoln laughed at first when I told him that's what I drove, but then he made me feel at ease and said, "No, that's cool—whatever gets you from one place to the other.") It was actually very fun talking to Lincoln. I was learning a lot about cars, and we laughed and joked about how my Civic would do in a race. As we talked, Lincoln blew smoke up toward the ceiling, so as not to bother us.

Then Ben's little sister Tracy saw us and came over to our booth. Right when she did, Lincoln blew some smoke up into the air, and Tracy walked right into it. She didn't know where it came from and looked around coughing and puzzled. Lincoln hid his cigarette, and Tracy stood there befuddled. We all got a great laugh out of it. I think it made Lincoln feel less embarrassed about smoking. When Tracy found out the smoke was coming from Lincoln, she was surprised, but seeing that Ben and I were OK with it, she relaxed and just started talking with us. Pretty soon, three or four others came over, and within minutes, Lincoln's booth was the center of attention. It was great to see Lincoln laughing and smiling, instead of sitting by himself. Several decided to go bowling after pizza, and Lincoln was invited. Several people fought over him to have him bowl with them. Occasionally, Lincoln would go to the back and have a cigarette, and the group would yell for him or send someone if he wasn't back in time for his turn to bowl.

I was pretty proud of my youth group that night. Instead of pushing Lincoln away because he was a "smoker," they embraced him and made him feel a part of the group. They could have easily treated him differently, told him he shouldn't smoke (because that is not what Christians do), or just ignored him because he was new. But they didn't let any of those things become barriers. Instead, they offered Lincoln grace. Grace that said, "We accept you as you are and love you—without trying to change you first." And that is living grace.

 ## MY LIFE AS A COVERT CHRISTIAN

That wasn't the only time I saw the effects of grace on those around me. I had been a youth pastor for several years, and I was burning out. I didn't just need to live grace for others, I needed grace myself.

I quit my job as a youth pastor and moved home to take care of my grandfather, who was getting too old to take care of himself. I was tired of the heavy demands and low appreciation I found in ministry, so after my grandfather died, I went to get a job—but I didn't look for a ministry job at a church. In fact, I pretty much didn't even tell anyone I was a Christian unless the asked me point-blank. I sort of went undercover. I had spent years working in churches, until all of my friends went to church—I didn't even know any non-Christians. I was kind of looking forward to being around non-believers (I think in part because I encountered too many "non-grace" Christians and had just become somewhat disillusioned with church people). I went to a temp agency and got a job as a courier—a document delivery person.

After awhile, our office hired another temp to help out with copies, filing, and to be my backup for document delivery. The girl's name was Jill, and she became my shadow and followed me for a couple of weeks on all my courier runs. She had just moved back from France, where she had moved to be with her live-in boyfriend. Things had gone sour in their relationship, so she left him there and came back to the United States.

I remember as we were driving through town on the way to a government office that she seemed to know every bar and drinking hole in town. "That's a great bar," she would say, pointing as we drove by.

"The Night Owl. Nice." I replied without interest.

"My friends and I go there every Friday," Jill proclaimed, just a few blocks down the road.

"Um, you seem to have been to every bar in the downtown area. Have you ever frequented any other places . . . say, *Alcoholics Anonymous*?"

Jill laughed, "No, silly. I'm not an alcoholic, I just like to have fun. Don't you ever go out?"

"I'm in my 30s and live with my mom," was my reply. I was purposely trying to sound like a loser (even though it was true) just to end the conversation. I didn't want to get into the discussion about how I was a Christian and didn't go to bars. "Let's just say you and I have different . . . values."

Alright, you have to realize that I'm not trying to make myself sound great, but within a couple of weeks, Jill had developed a crush on me. I don't know how or why. It didn't matter how short I was with her, or how much I dodged her questions about my life or tried to avoid her. She would still come over to talk to me or try to find excuses to follow me on courier runs.

One day, Jill invited me to lunch because she wanted to talk. I reluctantly agreed. It was one of those awkward conversations where there is an inequality of feelings. She told me that she had "feelings" for me and wanted to start dating.

I did everything I could to gently explain that I wasn't interested. At the same time, I was doing my best not to bring up faith or Christianity. I was so tired of how Christians appeared self-righteous to those who did not know God that I did not want to let that enter into the conversation. I kept dancing around the issue.

"Jill, let's just say that you and I are heading in different directions," I told her.

"What do you mean?" she asked.

"Well, it is like we are these two roads, and the roads don't meet. You are heading West, and I'm heading East." She looked at me funny, indicating she didn't understand. "You like going to bars . . . and I . . . don't like doing that stuff."

"So, what do you like to do?" I could tell she was being honest and genuine. She really wanted to know.

"I like watching movies at home, being with my family, working out at the gym, reading devotional literature, going to church . . . that kind of stuff." I was glad that she didn't ask me about church. I had been so burned out from being in ministry that I selfishly didn't want to share anymore. I did feel bad—it is difficult to reject someone who genuinely likes you, you know? So I offered her this consolation. I said I would be happy to be her friend, and that we could do things together—with groups of friends.

So for a few weeks we did stuff with friends and other couriers that we knew. We would occasionally go to lunch and talk, but nothing more than that. She seemed to get the picture that I wasn't interested in dating.

A couple of weeks later, she called me. "On Sunday, I woke up and I had this feeling that I just wanted to go to church," she excitedly declared. "So I went. I found a church and went. I really enjoyed it." I was a little suspicious that she was trying to do something to get me to like her, but I told her I thought that was great. She asked if she could go to church with me sometime. I carefully explained to her that I still wasn't interested in dating, but that as long as she understood that, then she could join me at church next Sunday.

She met me for Sunday School, and we sat together through worship. It was raining, so after the service we sat in my car and talked.

"I have been reading the Bible," she said. "As I understand it, Christians don't believe in having sex before marriage, is that right?" I nodded to say yes. "Are you a virgin?"

Now that was a pretty blunt question. It is not the place of this book to go into detail here, but I did with God's help remain a virgin until my wedding day. So I told her the truth.

She bowed her head as if ashamed. It was as if she was realizing that she and I came from different backgrounds, and she felt bad about her past.

"You know that I am not, right?" I knew that she had lived with her boyfriend in France. She looked up to see my reaction. She asked me point-blank, "What do you think about that?"

Looking at her face, I could tell she really was sincere in asking. I don't think she had much interaction with Christians, and she wanted to know what a Christian would think about someone who had sex before marriage.

I didn't know what to say. It seemed like an important moment; at least, my answer seemed important to her. I knew what the Bible said about sexual immorality and adultery, and I could have easily said that yes, sex before marriage is wrong, and that she was wrong for doing it. But I also knew that Jesus spoke about grace. So I let her off the hook.

I offered her the same grace that I had been offered. I started to tell her the story of how Jesus was confronted with a woman caught in the very act of adultery. I explained how the religious leaders were trying to trap him, and how Jesus had said that those who were without sin should throw the first stone. So I told her, "Jill, I am in no position to judge you. I have told you that I am not interested in dating, but you are still my friend and I care what happens to you. You want to know what I think? I think I would say to you the same words that Jesus said to that woman—'Then neither do I condemn you.' That is why I am a Christian. It is because I have fallen in love with this Jesus—this Jesus who treats people with love and forgiveness. Sometimes it seems that Jesus offers grace when his followers don't. I don't know why that is. But if you want to know, as for me, I want to care the way he cares. I won't hold your past against you because I don't believe Jesus would. I am captivated by the way he treated people with grace, and I want to live out that grace too. There is grace and mercy waiting for you, Jill—Jesus looks upon you with love and open arms. So, here's what I think. Neither do I condemn you."

Tears fell from her eyes and ran down her cheeks under her chin. She smiled and sat quietly for a long time. Then she thanked me, and she went home.

A couple of weeks later, I was invited to see Jill publicly declare her love for Jesus at her baptism. I watched her be lowered into the waters and rise up to the applause of her new congregation—soaked by grace.

SECTION TWO
FIRE

mals have instinct—God has given them a way of life, and a specific way to fulfill it. Humans have the ability to freely choose how to make our lives happen, how we will live them out.

And so the story goes . . . God breathed life into the first humans, Adam and Eve, and they quickly exercised their free will—and disobeyed God. The consequences were traumatic. This rebellion meant they lost their innocence, purity, everything. They traded one way of life for another. On top of that, one of the consequences to their actions was that everything around them fell. The land was cursed, which made it harder for them to live. Everything from that time onward changed.

OK, so what's the point? The point is that there was a time when life was how it was intended to be. There was a time when everything was good. When human beings walked in the garden with God, and there was no separation. There was a time when God's will was done on the earth, as it is in heaven. There was a time when we were good, and you could see it—we were without selfish desires, without hidden motives. There was no corruption in us. There was nothing to separate us from God. There was no turning away and crying in shame. There was no rolling over in bed when we can't fall asleep because we feel deep inside that something is missing from our lives. There was no looking back with regret over what we had done— no nostalgic look over the shoulder remembering how things used to be. There once was a time before human beings were broken. And that is how life was intended to be.

It was the rebellion of humankind—in other words, our sin[23]—that separated us from God. That was not what we were created for—sin and separation from God is not what life was intended to be. Indeed, it is not the best life. Some who are caught up in that life may argue that the life of sin is the best life—or at least that they have found nothing better. To them I would say keep reading, and don't forget that you should not knock the life I am about to describe until you have tried it and tested it.

At this point, we may ask ourselves, is it all pointless? It's done—we're done—we are all fallen, and we live in a fallen world. Sure we were made good, but that time is over and we can never be that way again, right? We boil water to make it pure, or use heat from flames to sterilize. Sure, sometimes we create machines to do it indirectly, but the foundation of it, the element of it, is still fire. We have grown so accustomed to controlling it for our use that the power and mystery of it—and our dependence on it—has disappeared from our thoughts.

THE WAY OF FIRE

We have learned that the way of Jesus is grace. He offered grace to people in such a generous way it almost looks scandalous—like he was running roughshod over the law of God. We have to remind ourselves that he was really fulfilling the law—showing us *the way it was intended to be*. Which brings us to the second question. The second question, "What is the best life?" is another way of saying, "How was life intended to be?"

Most people want to know—what is the best way to live? What way will bring me happiness and fulfillment? At the very least, what way of living will bring me the least pain and fewest mistakes that I will live to regret? The answer is fire. Fire is the way. Fire as an element will show us what is the best life.

To explore this, we need to back up a step. All the way back to the beginning—the creation of the world.

THE FALL

Back when there was nothing, God made everything. He made light, day and night, planets and stars. He made this world, land and sea, and everything else. He made life. He made plants and animals. Then he made people. Human beings alone have the distinction of being made in God's own image, and so there is something special and unique about us. When each one of these things were made, God said, "It is good." So being made in the image of God, human beings were also made good. In case you ever wondered, when you look around, there is good in each and every person you meet—even when you can't see it. But there is a reason we sometimes can't see good in each other—we are fallen.

One of the unique things about human beings is that we have free will. Ani-

ON FIRE

I like the image of fire because it has passion built into it. When something is "on fire," it is completely committed, you know? You cannot be aflame and be ho-hum about something at the same time. When something is on fire, it is consumed by it. When wood burns, it is completely changed. The qualities that make it wood are burned away, and it becomes something else. The process of burning turns it into something new, and it can never go back to the way it was. Fire has changed it forever. It is transformed from wood to flame, to ember, to ash.

Have you ever looked at an ember? Think of a time when you watched a fire in a fireplace or a campfire. When the wood had burned for awhile and finally stopped burning on the outside, it would still be burning *inside*. The wood held fire inside of it for a long time after you could no longer see flames flickering on the surface. It may even look charred on the outside, but on the inside it glowed orange. Here was the fun part—if you blew air on it, it would glow brighter. It could change from a deep red warm glow to an air-inspired, bright orange-white. With the presence of a strong wind, it would even burst into flame again.

In order to understand fire as an element of following Christ, it will help us to first recapture an understanding of our relationship to fire itself.

We don't often think of fire as an essential element for living. Like water, we have hidden its role in life, and we take it for granted. In modern society, we think we can live without it, but we can't. Fire is an energy that sustains life. In ancient times, fire literally kept people alive with light and heat. When evening came, the people of long ago would build a fire, lest the cold of the night overtake them and they became ill or froze to death. The fire of candlelight brought illumination and allowed them to see long after the sun went down. Fire allowed our ancestors to cook food (this one we still see and understand, at least when we barbeque).

We don't always realize it, but fire is still with us daily. A furnace is a controlled burning that heats our homes. A light bulb is a controlled burning of a metal filament that gives us light. Our car engines run on controlled explosions of fire to make them go. We still cook with fire, and sometimes we still

Chapter Six

THE REFINER'S FIRE

What is the way of Jesus? The way of Jesus is grace. Grace is foundational to all of the elements because if we do not understand it, we won't properly understand the others. Without knowing that God is love, and that he always leads us in the direction of deliverance and blessing, then we will misinterpret fire and wind. Without grace, holiness becomes legalism and the movement of the Spirit becomes righteousness by works.

The foundation of grace that we have just talked about is vitally important to what comes next. When we talk about fire, which represents holiness, we must not look at doing holiness as some way of performing for God. We don't *do* holiness in order to earn God's favor. Holiness becomes our *response* to God's loving grace. It is like friends doing something nice for us because they care about us. We can be grateful and respond by doing nice things for them; there is a mutual exchange of loving acts between friends— a circle of love and kindness. On the other hand, we can try to do nice things for them because of our fear that they will stop being our friend if we don't act right toward them. It is a matter of the motives of the heart, but it is an important distinction. The issue of God's love is already settled. He loves us. There is nothing we have to do. Holiness is our response to him in love. We respond as his children who love our Father so much that we want to be like him. More on that later. It is time to explore the second foundational element—fire.

are marred and scarred, and there is no hope for us to be anything but mired in sin. But I would contend that is not the end for us. To think that we are forever slaves to sin is nowhere near what the Bible says is possible for us. In the Bible, God not only calls us to be holy, he explains how he will make it happen. Part of God's plan for us is to make us pure and holy in his sight. God will purify us. He says, "Be holy, because I am holy" (1 Peter 1:16). And the symbol of that holiness is fire.

THE PRESENCE OF FIRE

It may help us to understand that fire as an element can mean more than one thing. Fire is first the symbol God uses to represent his presence among his people. In Exodus, when God reveals himself to Moses, he does so through fire from a burning bush. Later, when Moses leads the people out of Egypt, God himself is at the front of the traveling nation. "By day the LORD went ahead of them in a pillar of cloud to guide them on their way and by night in a pillar of fire to give them light, so that they could travel by day or night. Neither the pillar of cloud by day nor the pillar of fire by night left its place in front of the people" (Exodus 13:21-22). So in the dark of the wilderness, God showed he was present among the people by using fire.

At another time, in Exodus 24, God meets with Moses on top of a mountain. The Bible says that "To the Israelites the glory of the LORD looked like a consuming fire on top of the mountain" (Exodus 24:17). So again, the visual representation of the invisible God is shown with fire. Fire equals God's presence among his people.

This idea of fire representing the presence of God carried over into some of his characteristics. In Deuteronomy, God's holy jealousy is represented by this idea. Fire meant not only God's presence, but his power as well. He is not one to be trifled with—he expects his people to follow wholeheartedly. "Be careful not to forget the covenant of the LORD your God that he made with you; do not make for yourselves an idol in the form of anything the LORD your God has forbidden. For the LORD your God is a consuming fire, a jealous God" (Deuteronomy 4:23-24). The power and consuming nature of fire helped to describe the single-minded love and passion God has for his people.

There are other places where fire is used to represent the presence of God. When God makes a covenant with Abram, fire again is used to show that God is present. When two parties made a covenant in those days, it was customary to lay out animals and birds that had been cut in half. Then the two parties making the covenant would walk between them (essentially saying, "If I break this pact, may what has happened to these animals happen to me"). So Abram lays out the animal halves as instructed. When God participates in this ceremony with Abram, it is "a smoking firepot with a blazing torch" (Genesis 15:17) that passes through the pieces, representing God (Genesis 15).[24] So is God a firepot or a torch? No, but the symbol of fire is one of the best ways God can explain himself to our human minds. It is one way God can show that he is present.

The symbol of fire captured the nature of God very well for the Israelites. The presence of fire brought light and warmth; it guided them through darkness. But it was also powerful. If it was mishandled, you could be burned by it. Too much of it had the power to kill. Fire consumes and changes all that it touches. It is something that should be respected. When it is present, it demands our attention.

So the beginning of the way of fire is a return to the presence of God in our lives. It is not that he ever left us; the problem is that we have allowed our sin and rebellion to separate us from him. It is as if we were there with the Israelites, and we could see the pillar of fire in the night—and we turned and walked away from it to go our own way into the darkness.

This imagery worked very well to teach the early community of Israel about the presence of God. But the image of fire also taught them about what it meant to be holy. As we have said, fire was known as a purifying agent. It was a good symbol to represent God's presence because God is holy. Wherever God is present, holiness is present too.[25]

It is important to realize that God is holy, and that to be the people who exist in his presence, we must be holy, too. There is an old phrase, "Like father, like son," which means that the children will take on the traits of the parents. As God is our heavenly father, we are to be like him—brothers and sisters of God's son, Jesus Christ. We are to be Christlike. If God is present with us, and his Spirit dwells in us, then we carry his holy presence with us wherever we go.

HOLY FIRE

The fire of God is a cleansing fire. "Anything else that can withstand fire must be put through the fire, and then it will be clean" (Numbers 31:23a).[26]

Another passage that shows this connection is Isaiah chapter six. Isaiah has a vision of God seated upon a throne. He is surrounded by angels who continually shout, "Holy, holy, holy is the Lord Almighty" (v. 3). In this setting, Isaiah immediately recognizes that he is a sinful person and cannot stand in the presence of a holy God—the most holy being. Isaiah cries out, "I am ruined! For I am a man of unclean lips, and I live among a people of unclean lips, and my eyes have seen the King, the Lord Almighty" (v. 5). Right at that moment an angel takes a live coal (an ember) from the altar and touches it to Isaiah's lips. The burning coal from the altar symbolizes a cleansing fire—a holy fire—that takes away Isaiah's guilt. The symbol is clear—this burning coal is going to burn away any impurity and enable Isaiah to stand in God's holy presence. This is a hint that our sin can be taken away and that God wants to take it away so we can stand before him. Indeed, this is the very work of Jesus, who is described as the one "who takes away the sin of the world" (John 1:29).

Again, the Bible illustrates this through the whole idea of the "burnt offering." Now some of this is pretty heady stuff and takes a little bit to explain or understand. Our modern minds don't really like the idea of sacrificing animals to God—it seems so primitive to us. But if we realize that God was trying to communicate something to his people in a way that they could understand—and in a way that made sense to them in their day and age—it will help us to understand without prejudice. There are several verses (Leviticus 2:3, 10; 6:17-18; and Numbers 17:18) that connect the offering made by fire to the Lord and the idea of "holy." Without force fitting these two, there are principles illustrated by the connection of fire to holiness:

63

    a) Fire meant complete and total dedication of something. If it was a burnt offering, it was completely given over to that use. The fire consumed it.

b) Fire made something holy because it made it separate from other "common" offerings. These were offerings specifically for God's use.

c) What was intended for God's use could only be in contact with things that were purified—things that were holy themselves, separate and dedicated to God. (Such as the Levite tribe set apart to be priests dedicated to serving God, or the utensils that were used in the Temple and had been purified by fire—only those "holy" tools were allowed to handle God's offerings).

Fire and holiness are connected. We can even think of *ourselves* as "offerings to God," and as such we are in some ways "burnt." We are used up completely by God; there is nothing left of us to be dedicated to anything else. We are separated for complete dedication to him, and so we are no longer used for common things. To serve God we must be made holy—like Isaiah, we cannot stand before God without being cleansed and purified.

PRECIOUS METALS

Which brings us to a key illustration of what it means to be made holy. It is the refiner's fire. A refiner was one who worked with precious metals, such as gold or silver. The refiner started with rough metal mined from the earth. It would be a small lump of the stuff, mixed with dirt, other metals, and bits of rock. You couldn't do anything with it until you passed it through the fire. (Who would want jewelry with chunks of rock and specks of dirt in it?)

The process of refining meant super-heating the metal in a small cup known as a crucible. The refiner would completely melt the gold or silver over a fire until it became liquid. This not only allowed the refiner to shape the metal, but the fire would separate all impurities from the metal, and they could be skimmed off the top or sink to the bottom. Many of the particles that were not gold would burn off or be separated and removed, until only pure gold remained.

The fire consumed everything that was not pure, until only what was pure remained. The Bible uses this to describe how God works in our lives. God is described as "the refiner's fire," and we are the precious metal. It is not an easy process. It involves heat and melting—and surrender. The Bible says it this way: "But who can endure the day of his coming? Who can stand when he appears? For he will be like a refiner's fire or a launderer's soap. He will sit as a refiner and purifier of silver; he will purify the Levites and refine them like gold and silver" (Malachi 3:2-3).

God wants us to be holy. He wants us to be clean. He wants to restore us and return us to how life was intended to be before the Fall—when there was nothing separating us from him. God wants us to once again be able to stand in his holy presence. That was how life was intended to be.

God fully intends to bend and shape us to his will—like clay, like precious metals, he will form us to become his work of art, his golden jewelry. But before we can be, we must be refined by fire.

THE BURNING TRUTH

It would be difficult to argue with the statement that God wants us to be holy. The Biblical evidence is clear:

> "You will be for me a kingdom of priests and a holy nation" (Exodus 19:6).

> "You are to be my holy people" (Exodus 22:31a).

> "This will be a sign between me and you for the generations to come, so you may know that I am the LORD, who makes you holy" (Exodus 31:13).

> "I am the LORD your God; consecrate yourselves and be holy, because I am holy. . . . I am the LORD who brought you up out of Egypt to be your God; therefore be holy, because I am holy" (Leviticus 11:44-45).

> "You are to be holy to me because I, the LORD, am holy, and I have set you apart from the nations to be my own" (Leviticus 20:26).

> "For you are a people holy to the LORD your God. The LORD your God has chosen you out of all the peoples on the face of the earth to be his people, his treasured possession" (Deuteronomy 7:6).

"Therefore, I urge you, brothers, in view of God's mercy, to offer your bodies as living sacrifices, holy and pleasing to God—this is your spiritual act of worship" (Romans 12:1).

"But now he has reconciled you by Christ's physical body through death to present you holy in his sight, without blemish and free from accusation" (Colossians 1:22).

"For God did not call us to be impure, but to live a holy life" (1 Thessalonians 4:7).

"In a large house there are articles not only of gold and silver, but also of wood and clay; some are for noble purposes and some for ignoble. If a man cleanses himself from the latter, he will be an instrument for noble purposes, made holy, useful to the Master and prepared to do any good work" (2 Timothy 2:20-21).

"Make every effort to live in peace with all men and to be holy; without holiness no one will see the Lord" (Hebrews 12:14).

"As obedient children, do not conform to the evil desires you had when you lived in ignorance. But just as he who called you is holy, so be holy in all you do; for it is written: 'Be holy, because I am holy'" (1 Peter 1:14-16).

Some of you, after reading those verses, may be thinking that this sounds pretty demanding. You may be wondering, "What happened to all that you said about grace?" I know that it may be difficult to see grace in all this. Remember that this has everything to do with family relationship. It is "Like father like son, like father like daughter." God loves us as his children and gives us grace to enable us to live for him.

The truth is that God wants to restore what was lost. He wants us to freely live in his holy presence again, just as we did before the Fall. Holiness is not only possible, it is what it means to be created in the image of a holy God.

In this fallen world, God's desire is that we be set apart for his use. This is a part of what it means to be holy. God has made us his children. We are loved by him, and as his children, we should look like him—bear the family resemblance, as it were. And in many ways, the holiness he imparts to us is love—his love for us enables us to love, and to love like God is what it means to be holy. There are two characteristic marks of those in the family of God—love and holiness. These are the two primary ways God is described—God is love, and God is holy, holy, holy.

THE SEAL

Let me give one more passage to close out this idea. It comes from Exodus 28:36-37: "Make a plate of pure gold and engrave on it as on a seal: HOLY TO THE LORD. Fasten a blue cord to it to attach it to the turban; it is to be on the front of the turban." These two verses describe one particular part of the garments that the priest who served in God's temple was supposed to wear. This was for the lead priest (the one who went into the Holy of Holies once a year—the one who was allowed to enter the very place where they believed the presence of God resided). This one part of their clothing bears particular attention. It was a sign made of gold that they were supposed to wear on the front of their head. The plate of gold was to be engraved, like a seal upon their forehead. The engraving read: HOLY TO THE LORD.

Now I admit this may be stretching it, but I think this was symbolic. I think that God was trying to communicate something to his people through this unique part of the priest's garments. I think God was trying to let us know that those who walk in his presence are stamped—sealed and marked—holy and set apart for him. Now maybe this is a stretch, but I think that all who chose to follow this way bear the same markings—maybe not on a gold plate on our heads, but in our hearts. To exist in God's presence, we must be refined and pure, and our hearts must bear the markings, "Holy to the Lord."

What is the best way of life? It is to be sealed, marked, and dedicated to God. God who made us, and knows us best, has a way marked out for us. Walking in that way is the best way of life.

This may seem like something so overwhelming, so difficult, that it would be impossible to achieve. We may ask ourselves, "How could someone like me ever become holy enough to bear God's seal?" We have to remember that our thinking may be influenced by the culture around us. Becoming holy is not something we achieve through our efforts, an accomplishment like some kind of trophy. It is something that God does in us. It is not achieved as much as it is received. There is a balance here, to be sure. As God works in us to make us holy, we must walk in that balance. God doesn't purify us and set us apart so we can return to common use. We have our part. But too often, we think our part is to achieve holiness apart from God's work— we make it our own work and try to use our achievement to make God love us more. But as we have already talked about, we can't make God love us more than he already does. That is grace. Our part is simply to follow in the way he has marked out for us and allow him to put his heart in us. As his children, we begin to look more and more like him, more and more Christ-like, more like a member of the family. We walk in the way of the family. We walk in the way of holiness—the way of the fire. As we are melted in his crucible as God's precious metal, our Refiner looks at us with all impurities burned away, and he is able to see his reflection in us.

THE PINE AND THE FOREST FIRE

The young pine tree did not know how much longer it could stay standing. It seemed like months that it had been fighting off disease, insects, and dry roots. Because its roots were exposed on one side, on one side of its body the needles had dried out—it had patches of branches that were brown and brittle. The insects were starting to bore deeper into its body. The fungus was starting to erode away its base.

The young tree was afraid that with weak, shallow roots on one side it would uproot and tip over. Yet it was also afraid to lean its weight over toward the dry side in order to balance. It feared that the damage caused by the fungus or insects might have already made its trunk too weak to stand under any extra weight on one side. So it stood as straight and tall as it could. It had become so preoccupied with these battles that the young pine forgot to grow in other ways—it stopped stretching its roots on the other side toward the stream.

The other trees had noticed that the young pine had not grown like it should. Whenever they would ask, "Is that fungus growing there?" or "Did I just see an insect crawling under your bark?" or even, "Hey, I can see your roots!" the young pine would deny it and give some very good explanation. But inside, the young pine knew it was dying.

It was about the day that the young pine came to this realization that things got worse. The tallest trees saw it first. From the bottom of the mountain there was a growing gray cloud of smoke. It was small at first but quickly billowed large and black. The wind blew the smoke up the mountainside.

And where there is smoke, there is fire. It wasn't long before the tallest trees were telling the others that they could see flickers of orange and red jutting out from under the thick blanket of black and gray smoke. The oldest and wisest pine gave the chilling news— "It's coming this way."

Right after the old tree said this, another noise was heard down in the valley near the fire. It was the sons and daughters of humankind. They had gathered together to try to fight the fire. Some were climbing the mountain to try to get between the fire and the pine grove. They had shovels and buckets with water. They made a line partway up the mountain between the pine grove and the fire. The trees took hope that their friends had come to their rescue.

But the fire proved too much for them. They broke ranks as soon as the fire reached them. The flames were three times the size of any person, and the fire was moving too quickly up the mountain. The sons and daughters of humankind barely got out of the way with their lives. They scrambled to safety and looked up at the mountain, which was now glowing red-orange with firelight.

The fire quickly reached the pine grove. First there was a wave of birds and forest creatures fleeing from the wall of heat and flame. Then came an unearthly quiet. The trees stood and waited. It was all they could do. And then, all hellfire broke loose.

The blanket of heat rose up through their branches, lifting them as if by a hot wind. The dry underbrush on the ground and the layer of fallen, dry pine needles burst into flame quickly so that in minutes the entire grove grounds were aflame. The flames quickly consumed all that would burn. Then the fire rose up, tree by tree, jumping from dry branch to dry branch.

The young pine felt the red hot sting as the fire jumped into its branches. The dry patches away from the stream quickly caught fire. The pain was unbearable. All the young pine could do was endure it, crackling and snapping in anguish as its branches turned to flame and then glowed red with heat. Its dry needles were gone in seconds. The dry branches and some of the not so dry ones burst into flame and were consumed under the heat. Only the greenest of branches and needles were able to withstand the intense heat.

The young pine swayed and bent over slightly when it felt stinging in its side. Looking down at its trunk, it could see the insect hole patches had caught fire where the insects had damaged its bark and the bark had fallen away, exposing the hole-pocked trunk. The insects themselves could not stand the heat and came scrambling out of the wood of the young pine. One by one they moved to escape the flickering flames—and one by one, they could not; with a sizzle, each one perished.

The fungus growing around the base of the tree began to overheat. As the heat of the fire grew more intense, the fungus shriveled and curled up. The heat was too much for it, and it quickly fell off the tree in small lumps. When it fell into the fire, it burned completely away until nothing was left of it.

Once the underbrush burned away, the exposed roots of the young pine caught fire and burned, until only black charcoal stubs stuck up from the ground. Everything that could be burned was burned, and only what could not be burned remained. The main fire traveled on past the grove in minutes; the pine trees continued to burn for hours and hours, and smoldering smoke choked the mountainside for days.

When it was all over, none of the trees spoke. The evergreen pine grove was now full of bare trees, with a branch here and there of green needles that had survived, but had curled from the heat. Only the green grass right next to the stream remained as an oasis of color on a brown and black landscape.

The young pine had one side that was entirely blackened and burned. All of the dry branches on that side were completely burned away—as if they had never been there at all. The patch of insect holes, now abandoned by their deceased residents, had burned into the side of the pine by a few inches and left a large round indentation where the burned wood of the exposed trunk had fallen off. The exposed roots were gone, but some of their stumps still smoldered.

A few days later, the rains came again. They misted over the grove, streaking soot down the sides of the trees. The rains dowsed all the embers and washed away the charcoal, soot, and ashes.

With the return of the rains, it didn't take long for the ground cover to quickly grow back. In fact, it was able to grow back greener and stronger now that much of the dead needles and underbrush had been burned away—cleared by the fire. The bushes and low lying plants grew back thicker now that some of the branches above were gone and the sunlight made it all the way to the forest floor.

The young pine couldn't think about all of the green springing up around it. It couldn't think about how the fire had saved it from the ravages of the insects, or that the fire had burned off the fungus, or that it destroyed the shallow roots and forced the tree's roots to grow deeper. All it could think about was the pain of the burning, and the charcoal scars, and that it somehow had to start growing all over again.

Chapter Eight

WALK THROUGH THE FIRE

How do we become holy? If we are willing to try out the way of Jesus, believing or at least hoping that it is the best way of life, just what do we do? What must be done to us? How should we live?

Holiness begins by believing that God wants us to have the best way of life. This is an act of faith. We must believe that God exists and that he is good—even when we can't see it. This means that we begin to believe that God's will is better than our will.

And that is the real rub, isn't it? To be able to follow in this way, we must be willing to trade our will for God's will. It is no more simple and no more complex than living out that line from the Lord's Prayer, "your kingdom come, your will be done on earth as it is in heaven" (Matthew 6:10). It is the heart of Jesus when he said, "Yet not as I will, but as you will" (Matthew 26:39*b*). But we struggle to believe that this is the best way.

CLASH OF WILLS

If holiness is so important to God, then why don't we see more Christians living it? If God asks this of us (and we can believe that he has the power to deliver it), then why is holiness such a struggle for Christians? Why don't we see more living examples we can point to in order to illustrate exactly what holiness is?

For years I struggled with this question, until I read an old book[27] that also asked it—and answered it. William Law, a Christian writer from centuries past, observed the Christians around him and came up with an answer. To the question, "Why don't we see more Christians living the holy life?" he said, "Because when they became Christians, they never really intended to live it."

They never really intended it.

Dallas Willard, a more recent philosophy professor and theologian, said the same thing. He called these "consumer Christians" and said that this has now become the norm. "The consumer Christian is one who utilizes the grace of God for forgiveness and the services of the church for special occasions, but does not give his or her life and innermost thoughts, feelings, and intentions over to the kingdom of the heavens. Such Christians are not inwardly transformed, and not committed to it."[28] The reason we don't see more living examples of holiness is simply because many of those who claim the name of Christ have in some way taken God's grace for granted. They never really intended to respond in obedience out of a grateful heart. They had no desire to surrender to God's will—in fact, they were perfectly content to go on living according to their own will. And so a version of Christianity developed where it was acceptable to go through the motions of church without being changed.

If we never really allow God to change us, never completely surrender to the will of God, never walk through the fire to be made pure, what do we become?

Soi disant. Show dogs.

Because of this, I don't think it's fair to say that we have looked around and, since we didn't see very many people living a holy life, declare that it can't be done. I think it would be a mistake to say that God doesn't have the power to change us, and thus reject holiness because it doesn't work. We can't really say that many have tried Christianity and found that it didn't work—it would be more accurate to say that many have found Christianity a challenge to their self will, and *left it untried*.[29]

I don't want to see someone walk away after reading this, saying, "This can't be the best way of life! If it were, more people would be living it!" I would like to have the chance to tell them that this *is* the best way of life, but we human beings struggle with making it *our* way. We struggle because we are caught up in sin and indeed, at times prefer it. Sin and selfishness have so clouded our view that we have a difficult time seeing that any other way could be better.

WAKING UP TO A BETTER WAY

I have a friend; let's call him Rusty. Rusty and I came to follow the way of Jesus at about the same time. We were friends, and then we both went off to separate colleges and lost touch. Little did I know that Rusty lost touch with Jesus at about the same time. We saw each other a few years later. I'll never forget the conversation. I was shocked, I have to admit, at how Rusty had changed. He talked about beer parties on spring break and a string of sexual conquests. This was not the Rusty I knew from church and summer camp.

As we talked longer, I asked him about why he had stopped living by the values of the way of Jesus and what had happened. He got really quiet. Finally, he looked up at me and said, "Your way is the better way. The way mapped out in the Bible is a better way to live. I know I try to make it sound fun, and it is fun . . . but the truth is, your way is the better way. Following God's way just works."

"How so?" I asked. "If your way doesn't work, why do you do it?"

"I like the lifestyle, I won't kid you. I like the attention, and all the girls made me feel good about myself. I like doing things my way. And partying is fun. But it is not a good way. I've had lots of sexual partners in the last few years, but I've also had to go in three times to test to see if I had AIDS. Those were some of the most uncertain days of my life. I never knew if my life was about to change drastically because of the way I had been living. Have you ever woken up one day to find that your choices are catching up with you? There was so much frightening uncertainty. And the parties are great—until the day after. Waking up and not remembering where you are or the fun you had . . . well, that is no fun. And getting sick all over yourself . . ."

I stopped him there. As much as I cared about him, I didn't really want to hear the after party sickness stories. I did respect him. There aren't many people who would be willing to share on that level and tell it like it is.

I'll never forget the way he said it, either. *Your way is the better way*. My friend was waking up to the reality that our actions have consequences. We can follow our own will to where our own will leads us. Or we can follow the will of the one who made us. There are consequences to that life too. It's just that those consequences don't make us sick—the consequences of God's way are peace and fulfillment.

YOU HAVE GOT TO WANT IT

I remember in athletics we had coaches who would challenge us with these words, "You have got to want it." They knew that no matter how hard we practiced, or how our skills improved, if we didn't desire to play at our best on game day, we would not win.[30]

Too often the problem is that we don't want it. Holiness would mean that we might have to give up some things in our lives that we enjoy, maybe even rely upon.

I found out the hard way that God really can—and will—change our hearts. It was a turning point in my life, when I started to get serious about dealing with sin in my life.

I had been a Christian for years and had even graduated from seminary. I was a youth pastor, teaching, preaching—the whole thing. I had even made a commitment to pray more than half an hour a day, every day—and I was keeping it. It was a great time of spiritual growth. All of my life revolved around the work of God.

Now I know that this may sound silly, and may not seem significant to some of you, but it was a very big deal in my life. You see, I was dating this girl and had been dating her for a few years. And this other girl came along, and well, I kissed her. I kissed this other girl while I was still dating the same steady girlfriend that I had been dating for years. Some of you may be saying, "That's all?" (All the women reading this are probably saying, "That IS a big deal!" while all the men are probably saying, "What? That's it? That's not a sin." Be that as it may . . .) It was a very big deal to me.

I will never forget the next few days. I knew I had to tell my girlfriend. We sat down on a couch and I told her what happened. That moment I will remember to my grave. When she heard the news, she covered her face with her hands and turned her back to me and wept . . .

The next few months were some of the most intense of my life. I had always been a pretty good person, but for the first time in my life, I realized that I had the capacity to hurt people deeply. I had sinned against my closest friend, and I did not know that I could hurt people like that.

A strange thought occurred to me. I came to the realization that my Christianity was a sham. It was fake. I felt like I had been pretending all those years. I know I had not been trying to fake it, but I might as well have been. My actions had been no different—my faith had no real, lasting effect on me—so when all was said and done, it didn't matter if I had believed or not. If I said that I followed Jesus and lived by his way, but in the moment of testing I could completely compromise all of my values and hurt those around me, I felt like no real Christian at all. There was no power in my belief. I was Peter *before* Pentecost—blown about by the wind—calling Jesus "messiah" one moment and denying that I knew him the next.

Fortunately, I had been creating a habit of praying. I realized, perhaps for the first time, that I didn't have the power to do this; it was going to have to be a work of God deep within me. I spent months—I'm not kidding, months— daily asking God to change me. Every day for more than an hour I would cry out to him, literally, to change me. I didn't want to live that way anymore. I didn't want to be that susceptible to hurting others. I didn't want to be that kind of man.

I didn't want to sin anymore.

And something happened. After months, I started to change. I noticed that my attitude toward relationships changed. I no longer felt myself "looking around for the right person to marry" (whether that was my girlfriend or not).

Instead I started looking at myself, trying to become a person who could be there for someone else.

I noticed that temptations that used to crash over me like powerful waves now only felt like they were lapping about my ankles. They no longer held me captive. Mostly, I felt a deep peace.

For months I prayed that God would make me holy—because at that point in my life I knew I could not live without it. And for the first time, it actually happened. I felt like God was making me holy. He was doing it from the inside out. There was nothing I had to do—except *want* it.

And that was the key. I had heard a phrase once, "Whatever you can live without, you will do without." And it was true. For years I had lived as if I could take or leave holiness—and I did without it. I didn't have it—my life had not really changed at all. But when the time came that I could no longer live without holiness, that is when I sought after it, and that is when I began to receive it.

Until that day, I didn't know holiness was really possible. I realized that the problem wasn't with God—God had the power and the will to make me holy. The problem was that up until that time, I didn't want it.

A SANCTIFIED DINNER PARTY

A holy life begins with wanting it. After that, there is a process that God takes his people through to make them holy. That process involves surrender. You see, the reason we talked about a clash of wills earlier is because it is central to the issue. If we do not will to be holy, we will not do what is necessary to pursue it. But more than that, holiness involves our will. Let me explain.

What I am about to say is going to be completely incomplete and is only going to give you what I know about this from my own experience. There are lots of brainy theologians who know tons more about this stuff than I do, and they will probably pick apart all that I am about to say. But I can only tell you what I have seen, and I am letting you know ahead of time that I am not trying to paint the whole picture here, just one small slice of a larger pie.

There are a couple of important aspects of holiness that we talked about earlier, so I will only briefly mention them here. When God makes us holy, (at least) two things happen. First we are **cleansed**. (Remember Isaiah and the coal to his lips.) One of the other things that happens is we are **set apart**. Both of these are captured by a big biblical word, sanctification—in one sense it means to be made pure, not divided or mixed. In another sense it means set apart for special use.

To be cleansed is pretty easy to understand. When you use cleanser to clean your sink (to scrub away all the dirt and residue that has built up, and you make that sink as clean as the day it was made), that cleanser is a "sanctifier." It makes the sink "pure" in the sense that it is no longer covered up by crud. It is just the sink, pure and simple. In the same way, when the Bible talks about us being sanctified, it means that God is going to cleanse us from all sin (1 John 1:9). Paul prays for this when he says, "May God himself, the God of peace, sanctify you through and through" (1 Thessalonians 5:23a). When God sanctifies you, you are clean "through and through." There doesn't have to be any part of you left out.

At the same time, holiness and sanctification also mean set apart for God's use, not ordinary use. Here is one way to think about it. At my mother's house in the kitchen, there is a cabinet of "stoneware," the plates, cups, bowls, and utensils that we used everyday when I was growing up. There are several of them that are chipped, some I broke long ago, others have cracks in them from being overheated in the microwave. These are the everyday dishes that we used all the time, and they show the wear and tear.

Now my mother also has some old dishes made of china, and silver forks, knives, and spoons that belonged to my grandmother. She has them in a glass cabinet next to the dining table at her house. They are propped up so you can see them, but they are reserved for special occasions. They are truly beautiful.

Imagine that for some reason, the President or Prime Minister, or king of some country decided to visit my mother's house. First of all, my mom would panic because she would feel the need to make sure the whole house was *sanctified*. It would need to be spotless. And if this honorable dignitary were to stay for dinner, which plates do you think my mother would use to serve them a meal? Of course she would use the special china dishes in the cabinet. They are the ones *set apart* for special use—for the use of a special person.

This is what it means when God sanctifies us. We are no longer used for common things like sin that chips away our souls. We are cleansed and set apart for God's use—for righteous things—for the use of the king of kings and lord of lords. We are now at God's service and useful to serve the precious world of people he created.

ASK AND YOU SHALL RECEIVE

Again, I'm simplifying here, but these were the ideas that helped me to understand what God was doing in my life when I was going through this process.

In my own life, and in the lives of others I have known who have sought after this, I noticed a couple of things that we all had in common. The first was taking the step of seeking after holiness, and the second involved in some way "making Jesus Lord" in our lives.

We can't make holiness happen. The work of God is not like pushing a button—God works on us in his own time and knows when we are ready for these things. It is like grace. We can't bring it about. We can only ask and cry out for it. But it is not magic. It is God, and God will do his work at the proper time. In my own life, this took several years. So for some of you, it may be better to mark these pages and come back to them later.

Now some of you may be ready for this, and some may not. But here goes: If you haven't done so already, ask God to make you holy. Ask him to "sanctify" you, make you clean and set apart for his use. Realize that when you do, you have not arrived—you are only beginning the journey. We have to be prepared to walk in step with the Spirit (Galatians 5:25).

I remember coming to this point in my own journey. I was thirsting to be completely God's. It wasn't long before I started seeing the changes that God was bringing.

HOLY SURRENDER

The other aspect of the process of holiness I want to talk about is surrendering to the Lordship of Jesus Christ. This is not the whole pie, only one slice, but I have found this to be helpful to me, to better understand what it means to be set apart and made holy.

Every time I have felt that God was working to make me holy, it has been accompanied by a significant surrender of some area of my life to the Lordship of Jesus. It was as if my life were a house. Jesus enters my life, and room by room, he takes me through and "cleans house."[31] Some rooms we work on early—some of the darker, hidden closets of my life take longer. First, I have to acknowledge to Jesus that they even exist. But eventually, the whole house has been touched by him, and I live in every room under his authority. As I surrender each room and it is cleansed by him, each room gets the squeaky-clean, lemon-fresh scent because he has removed everything that stinks.

This is another way of saying that I make Jesus Lord of every area of my life. Area by area, priority by priority, desire by desire—sometimes in large sections, sometimes by small pieces—I surrender my will to him and begin to live out his will in that area. The clash of wills begins to end, and I start living out the will of my heavenly father. As my will surrenders to his will, I become more like Jesus.

Take a bucket of water and a sponge. (Start with a damp sponge so that it is soft and can be squeezed). OK, the sponge is your life. Your hand is your "will," the decision-making force of your life. The water is God (or "God's will in your life" is another way to think about it).

Crumple up the sponge into a small ball, and clutch it tightly in your fist. This represents your will controlling all of your life. Now take that tight fist, and dunk it into the water in the bucket. This is like when you become a Christian. You are "immersed in God," completely surrounded by his presence. But as your fist remains clenched, there are still areas of your life that are not filled with his will—they are not under the Lordship of Christ. They are under your control, clenched in your tight little fist.

Next, just for a moment, take your fist out of the bucket of water. When you unclench your hand, you will see that the sponge has been gripped too tightly to absorb any water. It is still just damp, basically dry. This is like what happens when we are not surrendered. Our will is still holding tight control of our lives.

Push the sponge back up into a ball, and close it up in a tight fist again. Submerge your fist back into the bucket of water. This time, slowly open your fist, one finger at a time. This represents how we surrender to the Lordship of Christ—sometimes it happens one area of our life at a time. Once every finger has loosened its grip, pull the sponge out of the water. Now it is full of water. This illustrates how surrendering our will to Christ as Lord and allowing God to "fill us with his will" work together. As we surrender (let go, one finger at a time), God can fill us (the sponge fills with water). I described this as happening "one finger at a time," which is how I have seen it happen in my life more often than not. Of course, we could just open our whole hand all at once, and the whole sponge would fill up with water right away. But in my experience, we sometimes surrender one part of our lives at a time. And God faithfully, patiently, lovingly fills up (think "makes holy") every area we surrender to him.[32]

We are made holy for a purpose. It is not for the museum. It is to represent a holy God in the world. It is to be able to offer love and grace (water) to a thirsty world—but to be able to do it without mixed motives, without impure desires. We don't serve to benefit ourselves—that is not God's way. To serve God, we need to have undivided hearts (Psalm 86:11). To be pure is to be of one kind, of one mind—not split and divided and trying to serve ourselves at the same time we try to serve God.

It may take months, it may take years or longer, but God wants to make us clean and set us apart for his use. But he will not violate our free will—he won't force us. We will be holy and useful for him when we are ready—when we voluntarily decide we can't live without it. Then we can ask God to show us what areas are not yet surrendered to him. The prayer of one who walks through the fire looks like this:

> Search me, O God, and know my heart;
> test me and know my thoughts.

See if there is any wicked way in me,
and lead me in the way everlasting
(Psalm 139:23-24, NRSV).
The way that they walk is the way of holiness. It is the way of the fire.

SECTION THREE
WIND

Chapter Nine

KINGDOM OF THE WIND

What does it mean to follow? If the way of Jesus is grace, and the life he gives us is the possibility of holiness, and if we agree that God's way is best—then what do we do? How do we live a life of holy grace? What is the purpose of this life? What makes this kind of life possible? These are all questions we will answer by wind.

Our third element represents the work of God in the world. It is the symbol of God's invisible kingdom, the representation of the work of his Spirit among us. We cannot see the wind, but we see its effects.

ON THE WIND

Wind is air, and air is all around us. It is the atmosphere we breathe. We cannot live without it. Fire itself is dependent on air, and so is water.

But wind adds something else to air. It moves. It is ever-changing weather. It is this movement that makes it distinctive. Wind is the movement of the air around the planet. The earth is alive with the movement of air—constantly adjusting from pressure zone to pressure zone, jet streaming over the oceans and continents. Wind covers the earth.

Wind moves the clouds that bring water to land that is far from the sea. Wind fuels the fire, making it jump and flicker with energy. Wind changes the temperature of locations as it moves cold air from the polar ice caps and warm air from the tropics. Wind blows plant seeds so that they continue to spread and grow in new places. Wind makes life possible.

To see the life-giving power of the Spirit, we once again go all the way back to the beginning—the creation of human beings. The wind of God has been giving life from the beginning. "Then the LORD God formed a man from the dust of the ground and breathed into his nostrils the breath of life, and the man became a living being" (Genesis 2:7, TNIV). The Spirit of God breathed life into the first people, and it has been giving us life ever since. We live because the breath of God is in us. And from the beginning, the Spirit of God is compared with wind. In fact, in both the original Hebrew and Greek languages of the Bible, the same words are used for "breath," "wind," and "Spirit."

The breath of God. The wind of the Spirit. These are the ways that God describes his involvement among us. God is an invisible life giver who is actively moving among us. We can't see God's Spirit, but we feel it all around us, just as we feel the breath in our lungs.

Wind is the way of following. We follow the Spirit of God and join the work of the Spirit wherever it leads. It flows naturally from water and fire. Water gives us the foundation of discipleship—we are loved, and we serve out of that love. Fire gives us the character, the refining we need. It shows us what is the best life and burns away everything that is not necessary to that life. We are purified and cleansed, not for common use, not servants of self— but set apart servants of God. Wind shows us how to follow; it is the element that tells us what to do next. We are not blessed to selfishly hoard it. We are not cleaned up to be put on display. Water and fire move through our lives for a purpose. They prepare us to move out into the world. Wind helps us to understand the way of following. We are to follow the leading of the Spirit of God.

FROM WIND TO ACTION

In the Bible, the wind of the Spirit is closely followed by the actions of God's people. It begins in Genesis, where the breath of life is breathed into human beings, and what follows is all the activity of human history. God's Spirit sets in motion the people of God, carrying out the will of God.

In Ezekiel 37, the prophet of God is shown a vision that displays this principle. Ezekiel is first moved by the Spirit to see the vision. Then Ezekiel is shown an entire valley filled with "dry bones" (v. 4), the artifacts of an army long dead and destroyed, now motionless and powerless piles of rubble. Then the Spirit of God speaks to Ezekiel, telling him that God will put breath into these bones and make them come to life again. The bones are a symbol of God's people, who had become dead and ineffective. God is saying that he will fill his people with his Spirit and make them alive and effective for his use.

Ezekiel does as he is told and speaks to the bones. They begin to come together and form skeletons. Next muscles begin to form and skin appears and covers their bodies, but they are still lifeless. Then Ezekiel is asked to give this command to the dry bones:

> "This is what the Sovereign LORD says: Come, breath, from the four winds and breathe into these slain, that they may live." So I prophesied as he commanded me, and breath entered them; they came to life and stood up on their feet—a vast army (vv. 9-10, TNIV).

It is the wind, the breath of God, that turns this pile of bones into a vast army, and breathes life into them. And it is the Spirit of God in our midst that takes our lives and moves us to action for his kingdom.

Breath is not the only way we understand how God works among us. The Spirit of God is directly compared to wind in John, chapter 3:

> Jesus answered, "I tell you the truth, no one can enter the kingdom of God unless he is born of water and the Spirit. Flesh gives birth to flesh, but the Spirit gives birth to spirit. You should not be surprised at my saying, 'You must be born again.' The wind blows wherever it pleases. You hear its sound, but you cannot tell where it comes from or where it is going. So it is with everyone born of the Spirit" (vv. 5-8).

Here, wind describes well the activity of the Spirit of God. It is hidden, invisible. You can't always tell what work the Spirit is doing, but there is no question as to its power. You can see its effects everywhere. Even though you cannot see the wind blow past, you *can* see the tree sway, the grass move, the dust swirl. You see the effects of the Spirit everywhere. You can't tell exactly what is happening in the soul of the believer, but you can see the direction of their life change. The Spirit of God moves those born of the Spirit. Sometimes we can't understand it, but we can tell that the Spirit is moving.

Again, the emphasis of this passage is on movement. The work of the Spirit is active. It is going somewhere—we may not be able to see where it is going, but it is moving. It is taking us on a journey. It is actively leading us. We saints are the wind socks, the flags, that are blown by the wind. When you look at us, you can see which way the Spirit is moving by the direction we are blowing.

Another dramatic passage where the Spirit of God moves as wind is in Acts chapter 2. In this passage, the disciples are waiting as Jesus had instructed them. "Suddenly a sound like the blowing of a violent wind came from heaven and filled the whole house where they were sitting. They saw what seemed to be tongues of fire that separated and came to rest on each of them. All of them were filled with the Holy Spirit and began to speak in other tongues as the Spirit enabled them" (vv. 2-4).[33] The arrival of the Spirit is displayed as a strong wind blowing through the house where they were.

It is after this arrival of the Spirit of God that the disciples take action. They are enabled by the Spirit to speak foreign languages without ever having to study them. They become bold, changing from a fearful band hiding under persecution into active missionaries taking their belief in Jesus across the countryside. The disciples perform miracles of healing and raise people from the dead. When they preach, thousands are converted. *After the Spirit arrives, the disciples do the same things Jesus did*. The strong wind has blown them out into the world. The disciples are now doing the work of Jesus in the world by the power of the Holy Spirit.[34]

We see the effects of the Spirit throughout the book of Acts. But Jesus himself explained that his disciples would carry on his work by saying, "I tell you the truth, anyone who believes in me will do the same works I have done, and even greater works, because I am going to be with the Father" (John 14:12, NLT). Four verses later Jesus says that he will send us a "helper," the Spirit of truth. The wind of the Holy Spirit in our lives enables us to do the work of Jesus. He says that the Spirit "lives with you now and later will be in you" (John 14:17b, NLT). In fact Jesus, after he had risen from the dead, brought this to pass: "Then he breathed on them and said, 'Receive the Holy Spirit'" (John 20:22, NLT). The expectation is that it is our turn to do his work—as Jesus leaves the earth, he leaves the disciples with his Spirit to carry on.

A LULL?

If we have been given the Holy Spirit, why don't we see these miracles happening in our midst today? Where are the dramatic miracles that the early church experienced? Has the Holy Spirit lost power over time? Has the wind died down?

There are several explanations of why the church today doesn't look like the church of the New Testament. When the Holy Spirit first blew through the house in Acts 2, God was displaying his power to introduce this new religion upon the world. Once Christianity had taken a foothold, there was no need to use displays of supernatural activity to show that God was active.

It could also be that the Holy Spirit is working in different ways now. The Spirit is in us and works through us as people, instead of having to show the power of God in a grand display. I certainly think this is part of it. We are now the ones God is using to show his activity in the world.

So realize that even though the Holy Spirit may be working in different ways, he is still at work and wants us to move into action. It may not always look like it did in the New Testament. But sometimes . . . it does.

OUR POWERFUL HELPER

I can only tell you what I have seen. I can only tell you what I have experienced. And I have seen the wind.

I was a youth pastor in California. There was a man who started coming to church with his mother. Both had come to the United States from Romania. They spoke with thick accents. The man, let's call him Bill, had started working as a truck driver. He was not a believer—he only came to church to make his mother happy.

One Sunday after church I noticed Bill limping out to the parking lot. "Are you alright?" I asked.

"No, I'm not," he replied, leaning over with one hand on his back. "Do you think you can give me a ride home? I walked over here, but I don't think I can make the return. My back is hurting terribly."

Bill and his mother lived a few blocks from the church. The pastor allowed him to park his truck in the church parking lot—it was too big to park on the street in the neighborhood where they lived. He would often walk from his house to the church to get the truck to start his delivery route.

I told him it was no problem; I'd be happy to give him a ride home. I carefully helped him get slowly into the passenger seat of my car. He winced with pain every time he moved or twisted his waist.

As we drove, Bill explained he had hurt his back and had not been able to drive his truck for about a week. He was afraid he was going to lose his job. He didn't know what to do. He was helping his mother pay for their small house. He had visited the doctor, but the doctor said that there was nothing she could do for him.

As we pulled up to the front of their house, I felt a scared feeling in the pit of my stomach. I started feeling nervous, for no reason. I realized what was happening. I felt the Holy Spirit nudging me to do something. Bill opened the door to get out.

"Bill . . . do you mind if we pray for your back?" I was so nervous and scared. What if I prayed and my prayers were no good and God didn't do anything? What if he decided not to become a Christian because I prayed wrong? I know it sounds stupid, but those were the thoughts going through my head at that instant.

"Couldn't hurt," he said, half bent over and out the door. He stopped and leaned on the seat to let me pray.

I prayed short and sweet. I just asked God to heal his back if that was what God wanted to do. No more, no less. Bill said a polite thank you, and limped into the house.

By the next Sunday, I had forgotten about what had happened—until Bill came running up to me. He was quite excited.

"Guess what?!" Bill blurted loudly, grabbing my shoulder. "After you dropped me off last week, as I was walking into the house, my back started feeling better. By the time I got inside, I felt fine. In fact, it felt so good, I have been able to go back to work this week. I was able to drive my truck all day long with no pain. The next time my back hurts, instead of going to the doctor, I'm coming to you!"

It was a great moment, and I smiled with him. I quickly explained to him a very important concept. *I can't heal a man's back*, but I know the one who can. It was the Spirit of God that healed him. There is no power within my body or brain to heal a person, but I can pray when led by the Spirit and do what the Spirit is asking me to do.[35] God is moving all around us. He wants us to join him.

We follow Christ by relying upon the Holy Spirit to direct our lives. We should not allow our science-oriented culture tell our faith what is possible and what is not. We won't see the effects of the Spirit in our midst if we decide they are not possible and don't pray for them.

The truth is that we have been given everything we need to do the work of the kingdom. The same Spirit that breathed life into Adam, the same Spirit that raised up the dry bones, the same wind that blew through the house at Pentecost is the one that fills our lives and enables us to do God's work.

TOO BUSY

What keeps us from doing God's work? What hinders the movement of the Spirit? Our churches today are full of programs to meet the needs of people. Don't get me wrong, these are great. Many of our programs are prayerful answers to the needs of the surrounding community. But what if we have become so involved with church programs that it has hindered the Spirit's ability to lead? What if we have become a busy church, but no longer a Spirit-filled, Spirit-led church?

What if we have become so full of activity that we are no longer available for action?

Is it possible that we don't see the movement of the Spirit around us because we have stopped going out into the world? Have our church programs become focused on meeting the needs of our regular attendees and are no longer focused on the work of the Spirit to move us out into the world? Is the reason that we don't see the activity of the Spirit of God in our midst because we are so busy *doing* church that we have ceased to *be* the church?

I have been caught up in this myself. I have already mentioned that at one point, I became so involved with church life that I became isolated. I honestly got to the point where I did not have any friends outside the church. I was so busy with church involvement, that I did not even have any relationships outside the church. I remember our church had a "friendship Sunday," where you are supposed to bring a friend who does not go to church. I didn't have anyone I could bring. I thought that I might invite the grocery store clerk, because that was the only person I had contact with beyond my church life.

It becomes very easy to become insulated from the world by our busyness. We may give of time and money, but there should also be *involvement* with the world. I know great church people—godly people, who are constantly busy with church activities. Two services and Sunday School on Sunday. Weekly prayer meeting, Wednesday night service, and small group. Board meeting once a month. Like me when I worked for the church, all of their life and recreation and friends are centered around church. The only people we know or spend time with are people who are Christian and go to church. But is that what church was meant to be? When I read my New Testament, I see that the church was a tight-knit, supportive community. They were constantly meeting together to eat, learn, and worship. The church back then had lots of activity. But in those pages I also see a church active in the world. I see the Spirit of God moving people *out*.

The way we know God is calling us to go into the world is by listening to his Spirit. If we do not rely upon the Spirit of God to direct us as much as we rely on breath, then we have put God in the back seat and we are driving our lives. What does it mean to follow? It means to rely upon God's Spirit like breathing.

MINI MISSIONS

One of the ways churches and youth groups have moved into the world is through mission trips. Mission trips are great, and they teach us a great deal about the world. Here's how it goes. The youth group raises money and goes on the mission trip or service project. Then they come back to report what they did to the church. Everyone is excited to hear the stories. So the teenagers get up in front of the church to testify. And here is what they say: "We went there to minister, but they ministered to us more than we did to them. We were there with those people, and they were poor . . . they had nothing . . . and it just made me so grateful for everything I have."

I understand what they are trying to say, and gratefulness should be a part of us as we are active in the world. But in many ways, when we say this, we have missed the point.

The point of the mission trip is not to make us feel thankful for all that we have. It is not about us. If we see someone suffering, and we come back happy that we are not suffering, we have missed it. We don't go to other cultures and visit the poor so that we can go right back to living exactly the way we were living before the trip. That is not what it means to be led by the Spirit. We should go and see the needs of the world, and then allow the Holy Spirit to lead us to action. When we see others in need, it should move us to change our lifestyle, to hear the Spirit calling us to be involved in serving with our lives—whether we are on a mission trip or not. When we do go into the world to serve, we should hear the voice of the Spirit of God calling us to a lifestyle of ministry from a Christlike heart.

HOLY SPIRIT LEADING

We can hide in our churches like caves. We can check service off our list and be done with it. Or we can stand in the wind.

Water and fire have prepared us for what comes next. To live in the kingdom of the wind, we stand on the foundation of grace, and we become cleansed and surrendered. All there is left to do is let the Spirit lead us. Think about it. We are talking about the basics of the basics of discipleship. We are talking about the core of the core—the key questions. When we boil down the Christian life to its most foundational essence, we have this: The way of Jesus is grace. The best life is the life of holiness, free from sin, cleansed before God and set apart for his use. To follow means we let the Spirit lead us.

There is no more to add to it than that. If you were ever confused about what you are supposed to do or be as a Christian, that is it. You are to live out the grace and love of Jesus, walk in holiness before God, and let his Spirit direct your life and give you purpose through participating in the kingdom.

I'll end this chapter with a Bible verse has had tremendous impact on me. A college friend shared it with me, and it has always kept me on track. It is Hebrews 3:7-8: "So as the Holy Spirit says, 'Today if you hear his voice, do not harden your hearts as you did in the rebellion . . .'"

Today, if you hear the voice of the Holy Spirit, don't turn away. Listen. Constantly practice discerning the voice of the Holy Spirit among all of the other voices that clamor for your attention. Learn to hear the sound of the Spirit's voice, and then don't harden your heart against it. If the Spirit is asking you to do something, simply do it. Don't question, don't hesitate. Merely obey. Trust enough by faith that God loves you and will never leave you or abandon you. He won't ask you to do something and then leave you stranded, scrambling for strength—he will be with you. If you do this, you won't go astray. The culture around you won't be able to trip you up and distract you into going the wrong direction. With this element in place, not even the Christian cultures that we set up will be able to distract or isolate us. Keep your heart soft before God, and the ear of your heart open to him. Learn to hear the sound of the wind.

THE PINE AND THE MIGHTY WIND

Growth in the grove seemed to happen faster after the fire. The new green around the floor of the pine grove began to spread here and there over the ground, which was black from the burning. The cleared black forest floor made it easy for seeds to sprout up wherever they fell. All of the weeds were gone now—they burned up quickly in the fire—and the forest plants were returning in great number.

The young pine began to grow again too. It still had large scars from the fire, but there were no more insects or fungus or dry root to stop it. It drew water from the stream, and it was quickly becoming one of the tallest trees in the grove. The young pine noticed that the birds and forest creatures had returned. Even the sons and daughters of humankind came back to see the forest. They looked and pointed at the blackened branches and the charcoal markings on the trees. One or two of them even climbed up on some of the lower branches that had not burned away. This was always a great delight to the trees, to be noticed and climbed by humankind.

As the young pine grew, new limbs started to grow out around the side where its branches had burned away. Its other limbs grew new green needles that absorbed the sunlight. The young pine matured and grew tall and wide with new branches on every side.

One day, pinecones began to sprout from several of the young pine's branches. The whole grove celebrated the arrival of the pinecones. The older trees gave thanks for the pinecones—the fruit of the pine tree. The cones were indeed the fruit of these evergreens, and they carried in them the seeds of future generations of pine trees. It was the way that the grove would continue to thrive and expand.

One day, the tallest tree in the grove reported seeing dark clouds at the far end of the valley. A large storm was blowing in across the valley toward the mountain. Soon the valley was dark and covered by clouds. Slowly at first, all of the trees in the grove began to sway—moved by an invisible force. They could hear a rustling of pine needles and a whirring sound of movement through their branches. The sounds got louder, and the trees began to sway farther and faster.

A strong wind was blowing up from the valley, all the way over the top of the mountain. The storm moved closer and reached the bottom of the mountain. By that time, the wind was blowing full force up the mountainside. The young pine dug hard into the ground with its roots. The wind rocked the tree back and forth, bending it side to side, up and down. All of its branches bent away under the strength of the wind. Some of the smaller branches snapped under the strain and flew up the mountain, tumbling in a hurried roll and flying away.

The pinecones bounced around their branches, swinging back and forth. Most of the cones weighed too much to stay attached through such a powerful wind, and they broke off. The young pine saw several blow uphill, landing just past the farthest edge of the grove. "My pinecones!" the young pine exclaimed, curved almost halfway over from a strong blast of air.

"Do not worry, young pine!" the tallest one yelled back down into the wind. "The fruit you bear must yield itself to the mighty wind. It must follow the wind wherever it blows."

The dark clouds rolled quickly overhead, and the pine trees bent and swung, switched and fluttered here and there at the wind's command. The force of the trees bending down and then back up caused more pinecones to fling far outside the grove, much like when a bow bends and then snaps quickly back to shoot an arrow. After a time, the storm moved over the mountaintop, and the wind subsided.

When some of the dust settled, the young pine looked around to see where its pinecones had gone. It could just barely see one that had flown up the mountainside, outside the safety of the grove. The young pine strained to see what had happened to its little cone. It had come to rest in an open space, wedged next to a rock. "Oh, my little pinecone. How I wish you had fallen here next to me so that I could take care of you."

Day after day, the young pine stretched to see how its little pinecone was doing out in the open up the mountainside. One day it looked to see, and the pinecone was gone. It was no longer wedged between the rocks. The young pine asked the tallest tree what had happened, and the tall tree said that a strong wind in the night had come and carried the pinecone away. "But look, young one," said the tall tree, "all is not lost. Look there between the rocks where the pinecone had been."

The young pine strained to see. There, where the pinecone had been, between the rocks was a seedling—a tiny little pine tree, growing up from the rocks, far beyond the grove.

"There you see, young one," continued the tallest pine, "there is the beginning of a new pine grove. The wind has done what we could not. As the ancient ones have said, 'You can count the number of seeds in the apple, but not the number of apples in the seed.'"

THE BREATH OF GOD IN US

Breathe deep. Breathe deep, for God has sent his Spirit over us like the wind. The Spirit is moving over the earth, and God is moving us to where he is at work. He calls us to join him—to participate with him in the kingdom.

The Spirit is wind; it is the breath of God that covers the earth. It is a picture of power and intimacy. God is moving in our midst with the strength of a mighty wind, and yet, he is as close and gentle as the breath of air in our lungs. It is fitting for the one who is love, and who loves the world, to portray his Spirit as something that covers the earth. The Spirit's love is active and moving among us, like breath in our lungs.

GOD USES US

God is moving over the whole earth, building his kingdom. His will is being done on earth as it is in heaven. His Spirit is active. However, as God builds his kingdom in this world, he doesn't do it alone.

God consistently uses his creation to further his will and join him in his work. We keep going back and talking about the first chapters in Genesis—the creation of the world and humankind. God created everything there is—once. After that, he uses his creation to complete his will for the world. (The elements we are looking at are examples of this—God first created water, fire and wind, then God uses them to show us about himself.) God makes something, then uses that thing to show his glory. The Bible speaks about nature in this way.

God doesn't speak about his greatness—his creation does, "the heavens declare the glory of God" (Psalm 19:1). God created angels, and then used the angels to send his messages to people. God made people, and now he calls upon his people to participate in the building of his kingdom.

God uses us. He used Moses to lead his people. He raised up prophets to communicate to the nations. He used the early church to spread the message of his love throughout the earth. And he calls upon his church today to be his hands to the world.

If God's kingdom will come, and his will be done, it will be done through us.

WIND DIRECTED

What does it mean to follow? How do we follow God in an elemental way, stripped of all the Christian cultural trappings that keep us from the real Christian life—the way it was meant to be lived? If God wants to use us to do his will, it is vitally important that we are attentive to his Spirit. We have to live in such a way that we are watching and listening for God's Spirit to tell us exactly what his will is. Only then will we be able to do it.

How do we know what God's will is? We know from the Bible—God has spoken to us through his word. But we also know from prayer. God still speaks to us today through ongoing conversation with him in prayer.

I mentioned before that at one time in my life I made a commitment to pray every day for more than half an hour a day. I found that the more time I spent consistently in prayer, the more I found God talking back and answering. When I took more time to pray, it stopped being an exercise of rattling off my grocery list of needs to him and then going on with my day. The more I prayed, the more it became like a conversation. When I would pray for more than ten minutes, I was quickly done with my list in the first minute. Then I would just spend time with him. I would worship him, praise him, give thanks to him—and just talk with him. Sometimes I would just sit in silence. I used to call it, "wasting time with God." I set a time to meet, and instead of leaving early, if I ran out of things to say, I would just stay in an attitude of prayer and spend time with God, like sitting with a friend at a coffee shop. Sometimes we would talk, sometimes we would sit quietly together.

The more I did this, the more I found that God actually would speak back. Prayer changed from a one-way list of demands to make my life better, to a two-way conversation. God told me many things during that time. As I allowed him, God's Spirit began to direct my life. OK, don't freak out because this idea may seem weird, but as I prayed, God would direct my life in large and small ways. I remember praying about whether or not to take a job. I clearly felt like God was pointing me in a specific direction.

But there was more to it than that. The more I prayed, the more I began to be changed. God began to shape the desires of my heart and the direction of my life to follow closely what he was doing in the world around me.

LISTENING TO THE SPIRIT

I saw an amazing example of this a few years ago. I was going to school full time and living off of school loans. I worked part time at a church to make ends meet—and because I enjoyed it. There was a Korean church that met on Sunday afternoon, and we shared the church building. The Korean pastor asked me if I would stay around on Sundays and lead an English worship service for the youth, who grew up in the United States and did not speak Korean. This included the pastor's own teenage children, and some children of other board members. They said they would pay me a few dollars a week for an hour-long service. I agreed, mostly because I could use the money.

A couple of months later, I ran out of money. I had to go to the eye doctor to get new glasses, and the appointment cost $200. I didn't have it. My insurance didn't cover it. I went to the school to see if I would get any more loans, and they said that I had taken out the maximum I could under the law. I paid the bill with what money I had—I pulled it out of my rent and food money. So basically, within a month, I was going to run out of money, and either lose my place to live, or have to stop eating—or both.

I was pretty desperate. I didn't know what to do next, so I prayed. I literally locked myself in a basement every night for a week. I called out to God to help me. I remember praying specifically—"God, I need $200." I know, I know, I have talked about how in prayer we move away from a grocery list approach—but that doesn't mean we don't have needs. I had exhausted my options, and I didn't know what else to do but take it up in my conversation with my heavenly father. This time, my list had only one item on it—money. I was pretty direct.

I went to church that Sunday, taught Sunday School, and then stayed for the Korean youth service. We sang, and I preached. Afterward, I looked for the Korean pastor to see if I could get paid for that week.

I ran into the pastor on the sidewalk outside the church. He was heading to his car. "Pastor, did the church happen to send me a check for this week?" As best as I could remember, the check would have been for about twenty-five or fifty dollars. It wasn't enough, but every little bit would help, I figured. I did not mention my need to any of the youth, or the pastor, or anyone else at the church. I thought I would just collect what I had earned and figure something out.

"Yes," he said, "I checked with my board, and they mailed the check to your apartment already."

"Thank you so much." I relaxed a little bit knowing that there was some money on the way.

"How did things go with the youth today?" the pastor asked.

"Fine, fine. It was a good service." He nodded. I honestly couldn't remember how it had gone. I was so preoccupied with wondering how I was going to take care of my finances.

The pastor politely said good-bye, gathered his children, and got into their car. I got into my car and followed them out of the parking lot. We pulled out into the busy street.

The pastor's car ahead of me abruptly pulled into the turn lane. He spun the car around quickly, making a U-turn back toward the church. As he went past, he waved for me to follow him. I didn't know what was happening, but I slowly made the same U-turn and pulled back into the church parking lot.

We both got out and the pastor walked over to me.

"Wait here," he said. "I want to talk to my deacons and board members about you." Then he walked briskly up into the church and disappeared.

I wondered what was wrong. The only thing I could figure was that his teens had told him about the service that day, and I guessed that things didn't go as well as I had thought. Great. Not only was I out of money, but I was probably about to get fired from a job. What else could go wrong?

The Korean pastor reappeared a few minutes later. He walked right up to me and handed me an envelope. The words he spoke I will never forget.

"This is a gift for you from the Holy Spirit," he said.

I said thank you and went back to my car. I opened the envelope, and inside was $200 in cash.

The point I want you to catch from this story is not that God answered my prayer, although he did. God completely met my need that day, and I honor him. But that is not the amazing part to me. The amazing part to me is how the *Holy Spirit directed that pastor*. The Korean pastor was so in touch with the Holy Spirit that the Spirit could direct him to turn his car around in the middle of the street. The Spirit could tell him to go back and take care of a need in the world around him—and he would. (And he did.)

That is what it means to follow. That is what it means to stand in the wind. That is what it means to have the breath of God in you.

INDIVIDUAL OR COMMUNITY?

The way we have been talking about this up to this point is dangerous. It is dangerous because of the ways we have twisted and distorted our faith, and we could easily make a mistake here. We could easily make prayer a personal thing that is for "me"—a personal, individual experience. But I think this is one of those layers, one of those ways that we cover up the true elemental way of following. God doesn't just speak to *me* about *my* stuff, as if the world revolved around *me*. We can easily think that way, but it is far from the truth. To ask, "What is God's will for *my* life" is the wrong question.[36] God is the lord of the whole earth. God's will for me is not separated from God's will for the rest of the world. In fact, it is quite the opposite. God's will for me as an individual is very much related to God's will for the community around me, and God's will for the world. It is the Spirit of God that shapes my heart to care about the cares of God's heart. The Spirit moves me out into the world to be used of God so that his will would be done to care for the people of the world.

Remember, God wants to use us to accomplish *his* will, not ours. (This is why surrender is so important to being set apart for his use—we end the clash of wills and now desire to do God's will.) This becomes important when we talk about prayer. The longer we pray, the more we are changed, and the more prayer moves away from asking God for blessing—to asking God how can I *be* a blessing. Our heart becomes God's heart. We begin to take on God's love for those around us. We begin to take on God's love for the world.

MOVING INTO THE WORLD

When I worked as a short-term mission coordinator, part of my job was trying to talk college students into dropping their plans for the summer and giving their time away to serve God around the world. One of the biggest challenges was to get students to turn their attention off of themselves.

Every year I would challenge students' life plans. I would explain how they had all of their life planned out. First they go to college. Then they "get a major, get a job, get a spouse, get a house." The "Dr. Seuss-ness" of it always made them laugh. But I think, in part, they laughed because they knew it was true. They would have their life planned out, or at the very least, they were following the expected steps that they had been programmed to take from childhood. Not that any of those are bad things. But I wanted them to consider what happens when we get so set in *our* plans.

The challenge I would give them was this: What if God wanted to use them to make a difference in someone else's life? What if they had so bought into their preprogrammed idea of what was expected that they would have trouble hearing if God wanted to invite them to participate in loving the world? What if a consumer culture's idea of success (a busy job to get more money to get more stuff) had shifted their values away from kingdom values and onto self? What if their idea of what to expect from life had nothing to do with building God's kingdom?

What if the Spirit wanted to move us into the world, but it didn't fit into our plans?

For those students who would give up their summer to join a short-term team, the next challenge was simple. No matter what your interest, no matter what your skills, no matter what your talents—consider how you can use the gifts that God has given you to join God in building his kingdom. God has made each of us with different talents and abilities. The challenge is to figure out how to use what we have been given for eternal things.

Some people are good with computers. Why not use those computer skills to set up a networked computer lab at an inner-city youth center? If you are gifted in business, why start a business just to make more money for yourself? Why not start a business in Haiti or in the slums of Rio De Janeiro or Nairobi, where you could create jobs that affect the whole community by providing stable income for people living in poverty? If that is your talent, why not use it to break the cycle of poverty somewhere in the world?

I remember sending one of our short-term mission teams to Madagascar. We sent them to work among child prostitutes on the north tip of the island nation. In this resort town, parents would sometimes give their daughters to be prostitutes in order to make money to feed the whole family. We recruited business students to see if they could create business plans for new jobs. The purpose was to create alternative sources of income to provide for these families, in case these young girls chose to leave a life of prostitution. (I remember asking students to be a part of that team. I would raise the question, "What have you got to do this summer that is more important than that?")

Some are gifted in medicine. Why be a doctor in the United States, where there are 2.56 doctors for every 1000 people (or Canada where there are 2.14 per 1000)? If you are going to be a physician, why not go to Tanzania or Malawi, where there are only 2 doctors for every 100,000 people?[37] There are 100 times more doctors in North America per person than there are in those countries. If that is your gift, why not go where the need is greatest? No matter what your interest or giftedness, are you available to serve the world? What is the Spirit saying to you about loving this world that God loves? Is the life-giving breath of God in you?

I realize God may not be calling everyone to go halfway around the world. But too often, we make that an excuse so that we can hold on to our plans and do what we want. If we want to live by the Spirit, we need to consider how God's Spirit may be moving us out into the world. God's Spirit will give us direction—but we must listen. If we really believe that "God so loved the *world*" (John 3:16), then we must ask ourselves what it means to follow.

OUR HEART BECOMES GOD'S HEART

As we follow Jesus, we become like him. His heart begins to become our heart. As we draw closer to him, we begin to care about the things that he cares about. We love what he loves. Our hearts are broken by the things that break his heart.

So, just what breaks God's heart? We have to look in the Bible to find out. There we will find that God seems to care for those who can't care for themselves—they are in a position where they are unable to meet their own needs without someone's help. God calls his people time and time again to care for the poor and oppressed. He directs them to take up the cause of those who are injured and ignored. Consider these passages from the Bible:

> "Defend the cause of the weak and fatherless; maintain the rights of the poor and oppressed" (Psalm 82:3).

> "He who is kind to the poor lends to the LORD, and he will reward him for what he has done" (Proverbs 19:17).

> "Do not exploit the poor because they are poor and do not crush the needy in court" (Proverbs 22:22).

> "Woe to those who make unjust laws, to those who issue oppressive decrees, to deprive the poor of their rights and withhold justice from the oppressed of my people, making widows their prey and robbing the fatherless" (Isaiah 10:1-2).

> "Sell your possessions and give to the poor. Provide purses for your-

selves that will not wear out, a treasure in heaven that will not be exhausted, where no thief comes near and no moth destroys" (Luke 12:33).

"But when you give a banquet, invite the poor, the crippled, the lame, the blind, and you will be blessed. Although they cannot repay you, you will be repaid at the resurrection of the righteous" (Luke 14:13-14).

"Religion that God our Father accepts as pure and faultless is this: to look after orphans and widows in their distress and to keep oneself from being polluted by the world" (James 1:27).

Care for the poor and needy. Take care of the orphan and widow. Don't store up a bunch of stuff for yourself, but look out for those around you.

We have now come full circle. The reason we do these things is simply because God does them. God sends rain to water the land of both the good and the evil. He calls us to treat all people with that same grace. And God cares for those who are in trouble and who are in need. And because we are his children, he asks us to do the same. He asks his created ones to live out his will on earth. He invites us to be the ones to care for the world. He blesses us, not so we can hoard our blessings, but so we can use them to do his will. And his will is to care for those in need.

JUSTICE AND COMPASSION

So just how do we do that? One way that has been buried underneath our cultural version of Christianity is justice. Following Jesus is about sharing our faith so that others may know his salvation, *and* it's about becoming active in the world to care for those who need it. It is both. Following means we live for justice. As servants of God, we work to see that things are "made right" in the world around us.

Justice is simply a making right of things that are wrong, a balancing of things that are out of balance. It can mean giving appropriate punishment for someone who has done harm, or it can mean doing good where good is lacking. If someone commits murder, and they go unpunished, we would say that is unjust—something is not right.[38] On the other hand, if someone is poor, living on the street without food, and no one who can help does anything to help, that would also be unjust. Something is wrong. Things are out of balance and the good that could be done to make things right is not being done.

God asks that we defend those who are defenseless, take care of the needs of the poor, and take up the cause of those who are being treated unfairly. In other words, those who have resources are called upon to use them to bring about justice. If you have those skills, use them to help others. If you have money, give some to those who have none and can't make ends meet. If you have a voice, take up the cause of those who have no voice and speak for them. If you have power, stand alongside those who are powerless.

Justice and compassion go hand in hand. Compassion means, "to suffer with."[39] When we have compassion, we don't look *down* on others as if we see ourselves as somehow superior to them. We don't say, "Oh, those poor people—I sure am glad I'm not like them. I think I'll throw them some spare change then go back to all that I have." A compassionate heart doesn't work like that.

Instead, compassion takes a different approach. A compassionate heart chooses to suffer with them. Compassion sees someone in need and says, "I feel your hurt. Let me sit with you a while, and tell me your name and your story. If it is possible, maybe I can learn and understand what you are going through. Maybe I will even experience some of your suffering. With your permission, let me see what resources I have that may help you. It may not be money—it might be my time. I will work to fix the systems that are in place that are hurting you. I will work for your justice, and if there is nothing I can do for you, then I will be here to suffer with you."[40]

To choose compassion means that I can't be happy until you are happy.

Seeking compassionate justice means that we won't be satisfied with life when we become aware of the needs of others. We can't be content to go on with our resource and opportunity-enriched lives when we know that there are people starving to death, dying of curable diseases, or being mistreated. These may be happening halfway around the world, but we can't be satisfied with all that we have until they have all that they need.

In fact, we stop thinking about it in terms of "*we* and *they*." It is just "*we*" — as I begin to see those suffering halfway around the world as my brothers and sisters. Following Jesus doesn't make sense any other way. Jesus touched on this idea in the parable of a king separating his servants like sheep from goats. In the parable, the king identifies with those who are the hungry, thirsty, sick, naked, imprisoned, and outcast. He commends the righteous ones for taking care of *his* needs. But they don't remember serving the king in this way. The king explains that they served him when they served those in need. He identifies with those who suffer, saying, "Truly I tell you, whatever you did for one of the least of these brothers and sisters of mine, you did for me" (Matthew 25:40, TNIV).

ACTUALLY DOING IT

It is one thing to talk about moving into the world, seeking justice for others, and having compassion. It is another thing to do it. This is where we can see if we have been going through the motions and have adopted a miniature version of the way of following. If we are only talking about what it means to follow and aren't acting on it, then we have adopted a made-up, empty version of following Christ.

The Spirit breathes life into us to get us to move. If our faith is not active, we cannot say that we are following Jesus in the most basic, elemental way. Simply put, "What good is it, my brothers and sisters, if people claim to have faith but have no deeds? Can such faith save them? Suppose a brother or sister is without clothes and daily food. If one of you says to them, 'Go in peace; keep warm and well fed,' but does nothing about their physical needs, what good is it? In the same way, faith by itself, if it is not accompanied by action, is dead" (James 2:14-17, TNIV).

I have attended a church where I have seen faith put into action. I'll never forget the day that we gave away a car. That's right. The church gave away a car. It was an act of worship. One of the men in our church died unexpectedly, leaving behind his widow and their four young children. This housewife had to find a job to provide for the kids. She could not fit all the kids in the truck that the man had left behind. What she needed was a minivan.

Some members of the church heard about the need. Those who had money pooled their resources and bought a used minivan. One of the men in the church who was a mechanic used his skills to work on the van and get it running and in good shape.

That Sunday, half of the worship service was held outside. We all got up in the middle of the service and surprised this widow with the present of a car. She cried tears of joy and thankfulness, while the kids, at first wide-eyed with disbelief, soon began to celebrate, climbing all over the seats and honking the horn.

That same church has made a point of giving away one offering every month to a person, ministry, or need *outside* of the church. There are regular offerings for the poor in the community, other churches, and those going out into the world in ministry.

I have seen a youth pastor who turned the church parking lot into a skateboard area for the youth of the community.[41] I have worked with dozens of college students who went into the world, saw the needs of the world, and changed the direction of their lives to do something about it. I talked with one pastor who just couldn't take one more Sunday preaching about caring for others and then not doing anything about it. Their church had grown rapidly, and when the church board showed him the plans for their proposed expansion and new building, he told them, "It makes me sick. If this

is the vision of what the church should be, I don't want to be the pastor." Fortunately, the board was willing to move where the Spirit was leading. From that point on, they decided that half of all the money they took in would be given to the poor. They talked about it together and decided that they could save twenty million dollars by building a large outdoor amphitheatre instead of a building. They would give the extra money to the poor. They figured they would probably be a better witness that way—"Sure, we will sacrifice by worshiping in the hot sun or in the rain, if that means that the poor among us can eat."

When you break church down to its main ingredients and strip away all the other stuff we have made it into, you get the real elements of what it means to follow. It takes courage and faith to do it. But the examples I have given here are people and churches that have returned to an elemental way of following. This is what it means to follow as a church. This is wind.

CONCLUSION

There is an interesting passage about the "signs of the end," in Matthew chapter 24. Jesus relates how at the end, many will say, "'Here is the Christ!' or, 'There he is!'" (v. 23). But we should not believe it. If someone says, "go out to see the Messiah in the desert"—don't go. You won't see the real thing. False teachers and false Christs will rise up. Now I know this passage was not trying to say what I am about to say, but I use it as an illustration. In many of the ways that we have started to "do" church, in many of the ways that we have chosen to "manage sin," in many of the ways that we have withheld grace—we have created miniature, false Christs. When we point to them and say, "Look, this is the way to follow," the world doesn't believe us. They reject the miniature, false Christ that we show them—the one we have made like us instead of the other way around.

So if anyone says to you, "This is the way we have always done it," or "This is how we follow the way . . ." and what you see does not match up with what you read in the Bible—don't believe them. Reject the covered-up, layered, miniature, imitation, *soi disant* version of Christianity that they have created.

Then strip away all of that stuff. Remove all of the cultural baggage and "consumer materialism" brand of religion we have made our faith into. Get down to the real thing, down to the ingredients—the true elements of it. Rediscover your faith. Rediscover the elemental way of following. Dig down to the foundation of the foundation and I believe you will find that the way is grace, the best life is holiness, and the way to follow is by the Spirit. If you ever lose your bearings and have a hard time figuring out what Christianity is really supposed to be, then return to the elements. Immerse yourself in grace. Walk in the warmth and by the light of holiness. Draw your breath by the Spirit. Those are the elements of following Christ.

THE AXE AND THE ANCIENT ONE

Several winters and springs passed. The young pine grew tall. When spring came again, it looked like the young pine would grow taller than the tallest tree in the grove. It could see above most of the other trees. The young pine watched the little seedling grow and grow. Around it sprouted several other small pine trees from other pinecones that had been blown there by the wind.

One day in the middle of spring, the sons and daughters of humankind came once again to the pine grove. The young pine was excited that they had come. It was always a delight to have them climb up and sit in their branches, or rest in their shade. It would have liked to thank them for trying to help during the fire, but it did not know how. It stood proud when several of the people stood in a circle around its trunk and looked up, admiring how tall it had become.

Then suddenly, one of the sons of humankind took out an axe. The young pine was surprised; it could not believe it when the man swung the axe and struck its bark, sinking the blade deep into its trunk. Almost immediately, several more axes appeared, and the sons and daughters of humankind began to chop at the trunk of the young pine. It had taken the pine years to grow this tall, and within a few moments, the young pine had fallen to the forest floor and was being pulled down the mountain on a sled. It was loaded onto a transport and taken to a far-off place, far beyond the valley.

The young pine found itself on a pile of logs in the shade of the tallest tree it had ever seen. Nearby was a lumber mill. The tall tree was one of the grandest and tallest and oldest trees. It was a redwood. It was known as the "Ancient One," for no one could remember how long it had been there. They would say, "The rings of its trunk were too numerous to count." The sons and daughters of humankind saw the redwood tree and were so impressed with its size and age that they decided not to cut it down. Instead, they built their lumber mill nearby.

The young pine no longer felt any pain from being cut down. The only feeling was the sadness and confusion it felt because the sons and daughters of men had cut it down. In its sadness and confusion, the young pine called out to the Ancient One.

"Where have you come from, young pine?" asked the grand, majestic redwood. The young pine told the Ancient One all about the mountain overlooking the valley, the pine grove, the stream, the fire that had come through, and the mighty wind that blew the pinecones. Then it spoke of being cut down.

"Oh great tree, why has this happened?" asked the young pine. "I was soon to be the tallest pine in the grove. I thought the sons and daughters of humankind enjoyed coming to visit and play in our grove and climb my branches. Why have I been cut down?"

The great redwood answered from high up in its branches. "Oh young pine, do not be upset. You have been cut down for the sons and daughters of humankind. You will serve them the rest of your days."

"But I was cut down by them, not for them," objected the young pine, still bristling from the memory.

"Don't you know?" the Ancient One explained, "You are to be cut into boards for a floor for one of their homes. You will spend the rest of your days being walked on and bearing the load of a human family."

The young pine could not believe it. It was almost insulting. No more proud height. No more stream or mountainside. Now the tree would be cut and laid flat and walked upon day after day, year after year. "I thought the people were our friends. I can't believe they would treat me this way," it spoke in a wounded voice.

"It is a noble existence," retorted the ancient redwood. "You will keep the family off the cold ground and give them a level and smooth place to walk so they will not stumble in the dark. You must understand, this is what you were created for."

"Do not say that," the young pine brashly interjected. "Surely I was created to glean the sunlight from the heights of the mountainside."

"You must understand the reason for trees. You were brought from a seed not to be served, but to serve the sons and daughters of humankind. It is a noble purpose for a tree. You will provide their safety and shelter. You will be a part of their lives and serve under them all your days." The young pine grew quiet and just listened to the old and echoing voice of the Ancient One. "Indeed, all of your life as a tree has prepared you for this time. The stream where you drew your nourishment was given to you by the Creator—so you might grow tall and green. You have passed through the fire, which cleansed and strengthened you, burning off all that would destroy you. The wind came to further your work, and multiply you so that when your life was committed to this, others could take your place and follow you. All of your life, young pine— it was all for the sake of others. Everything was to prepare you to give your life for others and serve them."

The young pine was beginning to understand but did not say a word. The Ancient One continued . . .

"Remember who you are, young tree. You are a descendent of the bush that burned, but was not consumed—the bush that bore the fire of God. You are sibling to the tree that was cut down and bore the Son of God to his death for humankind. You are a cross, young tree—a life given for others. Your life is given for the glory of the Ancient of Days, the Maker of All, the Creator—and to serve his children forever. There is no greater life, no greater calling than to lay down your life for others. It is for this reason that you faced the water, the fire, and the wind."

NOTES

1. This is the Apostles' Creed, one of the earliest Christian statements of belief. I've changed a couple of words for clarity. In the original, it says that Jesus "descended into Hell," which can be theologically troubling for some people (why would Jesus go to Hell if he had never sinned?) so "the dead" was substituted because it affirms a core belief that Jesus really did die on a cross—without raising theological questions that unnecessarily distract. Also, "the Holy Catholic Church" was changed to "the Holy Christian Church." Catholic means "universal," but the term now has come to mean the modern (Roman) Catholic church, as opposed to Protestant church denominations. In this case, the word "Christian" is a more universal term for all Christendom, not just one denomination of them. (And sadly, as I contend in this chapter, Christian is a much more watered down term).

2. First of all, I am addressing the "Evangelical Christian" community, which is generally considered to be the collection of conservative Protestant denominations. When I use the word "Christian" that is primarily who I am addressing. The Barna Group of Christian researchers echoes some of these statements that this footnote references. Those defined as "Evangelical Christians" are "mostly conservative" (67% claim they are, compared to 30% of the U.S. population, and none of those who were defined as Evangelical Christians called themselves "liberal"), and 48 percent are affiliated with the Republican Party. (The Barna Group, "Evangelical Christians," <http: //www.barna.org/FlexPage.aspx?Page=Topic&TopicID=17>. Accessed Feb. 18, 2007.) With the rest split between the Democratic party, Independents, and other parties, then the majority of Evangelical Christians are Republican.

However, that most Evangelical Christians are Republican at the time this book was written is not the point. The point is that (evangelical) Christians have adopted a conservative suburban Republican image as their identity—or rather that they have adopted anything else as their identity except being followers of Christ. That is the point. We have allowed political parties, economic class, and culture to define what it means to be Christian, rather than letting our being Christian define everything else.

The other claims I have made I freely admit are personal and anecdotal—are Christians perceived as hypocrites? When the leader of the National Association of Evangelicals resigns as leader and pastor with confessions of sexual immorality and drug abuse, it is difficult to think that we are perceived as anything else. ("Ted Haggard," Wikipedia: The Free Encyclopedia, <http://en.wikipedia.org/wiki/Ted_Haggard>. Accessed Feb. 18, 2007.)

3. This sentence comes from my friend Rick Edwards, who reviewed this book and wrote that as a comment to help me summarize this idea. Thanks, Rick!

4. Remember this one from *The League of Extraordinary Gentlemen*, or the original story by Oscar Wilde of a man who remained physically handsome, but a painting of him continued to get more and more grotesque?

5. "soi-disant," *Merriam-Webster's Collegiate Dictionary, Eleventh Edition* (Springfield, Massachusetts, 2006).

6. Surrender may not be a familiar term to some of you, and it will come up again later, so here is a quick explanation. It is a term used in war, when one side decides to give up and submit to their opponent. Usually, when one side surrenders, they agree to live under the rule of the victor. One side chooses to stop fighting because they realize that they are facing a much stronger opponent and the battle is fruitless. This may not be a term or idea that fits with a "might" and "winner"-oriented society. "Never surrender!" becomes our battle cry, and we see surrender as something that only the "weak" do. But it is a positive term when used in the realm of the spirit. After all, if we

battle against God (or fight to do our will instead of his will) we are fighting against the most power-ful being in the universe. When we put things in perspective, surrender is a pretty good option.

7. OK, I don't mean to slam this lady and her dog, seriously. If she does stumble upon this book, I offer her my apologies here in this footnote. But I will not back down from making this point. So read on. Let's all agree, shall we, that we won't spiritualize our hobbies? I have nothing against owning show dogs (my mom owned one!). If that is something you enjoy, fine. Some peo-ple like collecting coins or stamps or comic books. But let's keep them in perspective. They are sideline entertainments, and should not rule our lives, particularly our spiritual lives (and we should balance our investment in them with a just use of our monies to care for the poor and oppressed). Let's not spiritualize thing like hobbies and try to justify our time by dragging God into it—at that point, we are twisting our priorities beyond recognition. It makes our hobbies the focus of life and places eternal things underneath our desires, commitments, and loves for trivial pastimes. It should be the other way around, no?

8. The seed and language of this idea comes from Dallas Willard, *The Divine Conspiracy: Rediscovering Our Hidden Life In God* (San Francisco: Harper San Francisco, 1998), 40. It is worth picking up this book and reading more on what real discipleship is supposed to be. The idea here is very important, and it would be worth going back to the sentence attached to this footnote and reading it again. Slowly.

9. Most people refer to the four basic elements: earth, air, fire, and water. Of course in our list, air is represented by wind. Also, earth is not listed. It might be helpful to think that we are the earth in this equation, as the Bible says, "for dust you are, and to dust you will return" (Genesis 2:7; Ec-clesiastes 3:20, author's paraphrase). These of course are not to be confused with Earth, Wind, and Fire, a funk/soul band from the 1970s (which I made a point of listening to while writing this).

Also, we recognize that these elements can also be viewed negatively when viewed in ex-treme. Water can mean flood, fire can destroy, wind can turn to tornado or hurricane. If anything, these instances remind us that we are dealing with powerful forces. Biblically, too, there are exam-ples of this—the great flood in Noah's day, the rain of fire upon Sodom and Gomorrah, the wind of storm that shipwrecks the missionaries. Because we are dealing with elements, the very basic materials of life, they are building blocks that can be used for blessing or judgment. In this book, I will be using these elements to symbolize positive aspects of God's work. The positive uses of these elements are present in the Bible too, and it is my belief that God's intention for all creation is for our good and blessing. God does not wish to use the elements he has created for judg-ment—but there are certainly there at his disposal.

10. From a T-shirt I once had. I'm not big on T-shirt messages, but I thought this one was important. I wish I had taken its advice with regard to laundry. I didn't keep the main thing as the main thing—I shrunk the shirt beyond repair and can't wear it anymore.

11. It is surprising to see how badly the Pharisees (and teachers of the law, priests, Sad-ducees, and others) had misinterpreted and misunderstood the law and faith and how twisted their religious practices had become. In fact, several times they had gone to the opposite of the original intent of the law. The classic example is the interpretation of the Sabbath law. God gives us a day of rest. The teachers of the law then added so many rules and regulations and stipula-tions that keeping the day of rest actually became hard work! God provides a day of rest—for our benefit. But the teachers of the law restricted and prevented good, beneficial actions on the Sab-bath because it would be "work." They ended up hindering the good that this day was intended to provide (see Matthew 12:1-12; John 5:9-16).

12. This is what gives the symbol of these three elements their power to illustrate. We can readily identify them. When water is present, what it touches is wet; when it is absent, it is dry. When fire is present, we see its light, feel its heat, and see the change it brings. When wind is here, we feel its movement; when it is absent, there is dead calm. This beautifully illustrates what happens to us when the spiritual forces these elements represent are present—and absent.

13. Our bodies are composed of somewhere between 47 and 60 percent water, according to the Rowett Research Institute, "Body Composition," <http://www.rowett.ac.uk/edu_web/sec_pup/body_comp.pdf>. Accessed March 10, 2007. We can only stay alive for 3-5 days without water. Source: "Survival Resources," <http://www.nhout-doors.com/survival.htm>. Accessed March 10, 2007.

14. In recent decades this has been seen as well. "In Ethiopia, the 1983-84 drought took the lives of an estimated one million people, destroyed crops, contributed to the death of animals, and threatened the lives of millions of people with starvation. Famine was exacerbated, if not caused, by war and failed government policies, but drought was the main catalyst to crop failure." (Tsegay Wolde-Georgis, "El Niño and Drought Early Warning in Ethiopia," *Internet Journal of African Studies,* <http://www.bradford.ac.uk/research/ijas/ijasno2/Georgis.html>. Accessed March 9, 2007).

15. Frederick Buechner, "Grace," *Wishful Thinking: A Seeker's ABC* (San Francisco: Harper San Francisco, 1993), 38. There is no question that this little dictionary book is not only delightful, but formative.

16. This phrasing comes from the *New Living Translation,* First Edition, copyright 1996. In the second edition, they changed this verse to read, "for the rains he sends demonstrates his faithfulness." The original Hebrew could be rendered, "rain for our prosperity." All of them are pretty close in meaning that God is sending rain for our benefit.

17. If you look back to John 5:1-18 and 7:21-24, you will see that the religious leaders directly opposed Jesus' apparent disregard of Sabbath laws in order to do an act of grace and compassion.

18. Philip W. Comfort, J.D. Douglas, eds., *New Commentary on the Whole Bible: New Testament Volume*, John Chapter 8, 1-11, from Quickverse Software, FindEx.com.

19. Some may want to ask, "What about the Old Testament, which set 'eye for an eye, tooth for a tooth,' as the standard? Isn't that God telling us it is OK to return hurt for hurt?" We have to take this in context. At that time, revenge and retaliation were out of control. If someone broke my arm, it was the standard to not just to break their arm, but to break their leg too, or maybe kill them and their family. It was an increasing spiral of revenge, so God set down the law, saying the punishment should fit the crime, "Only the equivalent of an eye when you lose an eye—no more than that." Punishment should not be excessive.

20. Some of this wording comes from conversations with my friend Mark Carter. I think he was processing some things he was learning in classes in seminary, so I'm sure that the thoughts here originate with one of them, not with me. The idea of being loved by God that enables us to love has also been explored in Henri Nouwen's *Life of the Beloved* (Colorado Springs: NavPress, 1994), and in Brennan Manning's *Abba's Child* (New York: Crossroad, 1992).

21. Of course I realize that by saying others "have not understood grace," it implies that "I understand it," or that I am somehow better than these people. I am not trying to go there. I am just saying that I have observed people who don't seem to live out the concept of grace as I see it in the Bible. What I mean by this I will explain further in this chapter.

22. Quoted here from the movie version, Rafael Yglesias, *Les Misérables*, (screen play) Columbia Pictures, 1998. Adapted from the novel by Victor Hugo, *Les Misérables*, public domain.

23. We have only briefly mentioned sin up to this point, so it may be helpful to explain what we are talking about. It is not always easy to define "sin"—let me try a couple of different ways that may help us. Sin is, in essence, unbelief. It is the opposite of faith, which is why faith is so important. For example, in the garden, Eve does not believe what God told her, and sins by doing the opposite of what God said and eats from the fruit of the tree.

Another way to define it is to say, "Sin is anything that separates us from God and each other." Where love brings us closer to God and each other, sin pushes others away and seeks to put ourselves before them. When we love God, we obey him, and put his will ahead of our own. Sin is to put ourselves first, pushing all others outside of our self-kingdom walls.

A third way is the definition of sin that Susanna Wesley gave her son John: "Whatever weakens your reason, impairs the tenderness of your conscience, obscures your sense of God, or takes off the relish of spiritual things; in short, whatever increases the strength and authority of your body over your mind, that thing is sin to you, however innocent it may be in itself." <www.tentmaker.org/Quotes/repentancequotes.htm>. Accessed March 10, 2007.

24. Of course there are other places where God is represented by fire, including the presence of his Spirit in Acts 2 as tongues of fire, among others. By the way, if you want to impress your family and friends, next time you are talking about the covenant made by walking between animal halves, you can tell them it is called the Suzerain Treaty.

25. This idea may help some of you who maybe struggling with the idea that "sin" somehow separates us from God. Think of it this way. If God is holy, everything he touches must be holy (pure and separated from ordinary use for God's use). So, impure, sinful things cannot exist in his presence—his holiness will not allow it. But his intention for us from the very beginning is to be with him, and so he has made a way to make us holy in his sight so that we can be with him.

26. I fully realize that the context of this verse is about making metals clean, not humans. But I want to show here the idea that fire is a cleansing agent—this verse shows this common practice. Note also the rest of the verse, that here and elsewhere in the Bible water is also described in cleansing—we recognize this too, every time we take a bath with water and not a flame thrower. Both water and fire have cleansing properties. Fire, however, also has a connotation of permanence about it—sort of a "giving over" or dedication of something wholly and completely. When a sacrifice was given over to God, it was burned—not just washed and left out for animals to take.

27. The book was from the 1700's, *A Serious Call to the Devout and Holy Life*, by William Law. To this day, the title alone gets me fired up.

28. Dallas Willard, *The Divine Conspiracy: Rediscovering Our Hidden Life In God* (San Francisco: Harper San Francisco, 1998), 342.

29. A paraphrased idea from the famous quote of G.K. Chesterton, "The Christian ideal has not been tried and found wanting; it has been found difficult and left untried" (from Quote DB, <http://www.quotedb.com/quotes/493>. Accessed April 6, 2007).

30. Faith is a part of this, too. If we do not believe that holiness is possible and that God can remove sin from our lives, we end up living out some kind of "sin management" faith. Our religion becomes one of managing sin, keeping it under control, and making up theological excuses for why it remains in our lives. For more on this idea, see the chapter on "Gospels of Sin Management," in Dallas Willard, *The Divine Conspiracy: Rediscovering Our Hidden Life In God* (San Francisco: Harper San Francisco, 1998). The opposite is to believe that God has the power and desire to remove sin from our lives.

31. I owe this idea to Robert Munger and his pamphlet/book, "My Heart, Christ's Home" (Downers Grove, Ill.: Intervarsity Press, 1986).

32. A version of this illustration first appeared in WordAction's Senior High Sunday School curriculum.

33. Don't get confused by the double symbolism of God the Holy Spirit (God is a trinity: Father, Son, and Holy Spirit) present in both our use of fire and wind. In both cases, they show God is present and involved in our lives in overlapping ways. First, fire shows God's presence and leadership in our lives, as in the burning bush and the pillar of fire from Exodus. Second, God's presence is represented by wind in his dynamic life force imparted to us (as breath) in Genesis and Ezekiel.

34. An important Bible concept is that the Holy Spirit moves among us as a community. Our faith is not just experienced as individuals. God moves among us as a body, a group. God's Spirit unites us, empowers us, and sends us out to witness and serve together as a community of believers.

35. Please don't misinterpret what I mean here. This is not to say that God does not use medical doctors or modern medicine to bring healing. In this instance, God chose to heal this man, and he almost came to that conclusion. But God has gifted doctors with abilities to use for our good. We should avail ourselves both to medicine and to prayer. It is up to God to determine what he will do and how he will do it. We should not shun medicine; the point is that we should not be afraid to pray when God is leading us that way.

36. This idea of asking the wrong question with regard to God's will comes from Henry T. Blackaby and Claude V. King, *Experiencing God: Knowing and Doing The Will of God* (Nashville: Lifeway Press, 1990).

37. From the report of only 0.02 doctors for every 1000 people in these countries. (Malawi having only 266 physicians in the whole country in 2004). Source: World Health Organization, "Annex Table 4 Global distribution of health workers in WHO Member States," The World Health Report 2006, p. 190-198, from <http://www.who.int/whr/2006/annex/06_annex4_en.pdf>. Accessed April 14, 2007.

38. Don't get this confused with what we have already said about grace. If someone harms you, they should be punished. That would be this "righting the wrong" kind of justice. But say you decide to drop all charges against them—that is grace that you offer this person. God is constantly being sinned against, maligned, and "injured" by the people he created—and God constantly offers grace to them, giving them opportunity to change and receive his love. So God desires justice, but he is also free to offer grace, love, and kindness to give people another chance.

Don't get hung up on the judgment aspect of justice. Justice may mean judgment—but judgment is God's job. Too often, Christians try to be God's judges, jury, and lawyers to the world, and we go around pronouncing people "guilty." Don't miss the other side of justice, which Christians often forget—how we should be going around defending the poor and making sure they get love, care, and blessing where those have been absent.

39. This idea and much of this discussion on compassion is at the very least inspired by Henri Nouwen, et. al., *Compassion: A Reflection on the Christian Life* (Image Publishing, 2005).

40. Not that things will be equal—they never will be. Sometimes we think the goal is to somehow help the poor get everything we have—then we can feel better about all that we have. But seriously, is that really a good idea, to alleviate the suffering of the poor and replace it with all the misery and stress of materialism and consumerism? The truth is, there are inequalities of economics in this world (the Bible acknowledges this—"the poor you will always have with you" [Mark 14:7]), but that doesn't mean we do nothing. We don't have to make things exactly equal where everyone in the world has what everyone else has. What we can do is make sure that people have enough to survive by properly distributing the necessities of life (food, clothing, shelter). In the often-quoted words of Mahatma Gandhi, we can "live simply so others may simply live."

41. Walking in the wind is dangerous—this youth pastor got in trouble with the adults at the church because the parking lot was filled with "wild teens" who took up parking spaces and sometimes smoked on church grounds. They said he wasn't paying enough attention to the "church kids" and was spending too much time on those "other kids." He was eventually fired.